SAMS
Teach Yourself Today

e-Personal Finance

Well Known on the 100 Club Christian TV Program

SAMS
Teach Yourself
Today

e-Personal
Finance

**Managing your money and
investments online**

Ken and Daria Dolan

A Division of Macmillan USA

201 West 103rd Street, Indianapolis, Indiana 46290

Sams Teach Yourself e-Personal Finance Today

International Standard Book Number: 0-672-31879-2

Printed in the United States of America

First Printing: March 2000

02   01   00   4   3

Trademarks

All terms mentioned in this book that are known to be trademarks or service marks have been appropriately capitalized. Sams Publishing cannot attest to the accuracy of this information. Use of a term in this book should not be regarded as affecting the validity of any trademark or service mark.

Warning and Disclaimer

Every effort has been made to make this book as complete and as accurate as possible, but no warranty or fitness is implied. The information provided is on an "as is" basis.

Acquisitions Editors
Betsy Brown
Jeff Schultz

Development Editor
Jan Snyder

Managing Editor
Charlotte Clapp

Project Editor
George E. Nedeff

Copy Editor
Sean Medlock

Indexer
Sharon Shock

Proofreader
Matt Wynalda

Team Coordinator
Amy Patton

Interior Design
Gary Adair

Cover Design
Jay Corpus

Copy Writer
Eric Borgert

Production
Dan Harris
George Poole

Dedication

To all of our listeners, viewers, and readers across America who have supported our efforts over the years to deliver practical and understandable information that empowers people to take control of their finances and make their lives better.

A special dedication to two members of our national radio team for their tireless efforts in helping make The Dolans *one of America's most-listened-to radio shows...to our Executive Producer, Scott Lakefield, for his unflagging commitment to quality programming and to Bobby Iorio, our engineer and creative consultant, for his willingness to go the extra mile to make a difference.*

Table of Contents

Introduction   1

PART I   Getting Started

1   What Is Personal Finance?   7

2   How Can I Use the Internet for Personal Finance?   13

PART II   Setting Up a Good Strategy

3   Budgeting—Planning for Today and the Future   27

4   Banking Online—Managing Your Money over
    the Internet   35

5   Credit and Debt—Taking Care of Your Liabilities
    Using the Internet   47

PART III   Building and Protecting Your Wealth

6   Insurance—Finding the Best Policy Online   63

7   Taxes—Internet Resources to Help You Keep
    More of Your Money   77

8   Investing Online—Growing Your Nest Egg   91

PART IV   Meeting Goals Along the Way

9   Family Finances—Your Changing Needs as Your
    Family Grows   117

10   Real Estate—Buying and Selling Online   127

11   College—Covering the Skyrocketing Costs of
     Higher Education   149

PART V   **Securing Your Golden Years**

12   Retirement—Planning and Financing Your
     Golden Years   167

13   Wills and Estate Planning—Taking Care of
     Your Heirs   181

PART VI   **Appendixes**

A   Web Sites Worth Visiting   199

B   Glossary   213

    Index   225

Acknowledgments

Many thanks to Jackie Day Packel, without whose valuable assistance this book would not have been possible. In fact, we finished the book just as Jackie delivered her new baby, Zoe… three weeks early!!!

Thanks, Jackie… and congratulations, new mommy!!

Advance Praise for
Sams Teach Yourself
e-Personal Finance Today

This book is a must-read for every person seeking to learn the basics of personal finance in the easiest, most high-tech way possible. Ken and Daria Dolan, who are highly respected experts in the field, offer us an invaluable Internet guide to personal banking, budgeting, borrowing, and most importantly, growing our investments. They give us common-sense advice on how to use the Internet to enhance our financial wealth and independence, something we all dream of.

In these times of increasingly volatile financial markets, your stock port-folios may have more to lose than you think. The Dolans will help you become an informed investor who can protect the value of your portfolio at all times. They show you the way to helpful and often free investment information that is available at your fingertips on the Internet. In my view, the Dolans are unrivaled in their wisdom, expertise, and helpfulness in the field of personal finance. They will give you the tools you need to make more profitable investment decisions, as well as how to protect your financial nest egg when necessary. This book informs us about an information technology revolution that is destined to profoundly change how we live, learn, shop, and multiply our wealth. We all can benefit greatly as we travel with the Dolans down the Information Superhighway to financial security and success.

Dr. David M. Jones
Vice Chairman and Chief Economist
Aubry G. Lanston & Co. Inc.

When I think of the Dolans (Ken and Daria), I envision two walking encyclopedias of personal finance. I call them "the first couple" of Wall Street. The "Mr. and Mrs." of the financial world. But in spite of their expertise and impeccable credentials, they are the most down-to-earth people you will ever want to meet. And you can feel that friendliness as you read each page of this user-friendly book.

In life and in the investment world, knowledge is power. More specifically, the correct information. And if anyone can provide you with the how-to-do aspects of money matters, I personally don't know any two people better than Ken and Daria Dolan. They expose the inside truths of how to make money, save it, and make it grow. Their irreverent (tell it like it is), but practical advice is more valuable than money itself.

Do yourself a big favor. Purchase this book. Find a comfortable place because I suspect that you won't be able to put it down once you start. The Dolans actually transform the once drab-and-boring topic of personal finance into something which is exciting and profitable.

In my many years as an investment adviser, I have met plenty of smart professionals. None of them ranks higher then the Dolans. None whatsoever.

Irwin T. Yamamoto
Publisher
The Yamamoto Forecast

The miracle workers of personal finance have done the impossible. The Dolans have achieved what no one else has been able to do: They've untangled the massive web of dot-com confusion that makes finding priceless financial information a daunting process for even the most Web-savvy surfers.

Their new book is a practical how-to guide that shows you how to harness the massive power of the Internet with just a few well-directed clicks of your mouse. The Dolans' "geek-proof" guide has not only unraveled the secrets of finding and using valuable information from the best financial sites on the Web, it also features a system that makes it easy for any Web surfer to categorize and customize data to meet his individual needs.

Gerald Celente
Director
Trends Research Institute

The king and queen of personal finance have done it again! Ken and Daria Dolan, America's best known personal finance experts, have simplified the online process and created an easy-to-use guide to maximize the power of the Internet. I am especially thankful for the roadmap on where to go and how to search. From beginning to end, the Dolans have successfully combined their years of experience and their knowledge of the Internet to cut through the complicated issues of successful money management.

Whether you are a new consumer needing beginning financial advice or a seasoned investor who has just discovered the need for extensive financial planning, *Sams Teach Yourself e-Personal Finance Today* is your guide to net returns. Don't delay getting your personal wealth and finance plans pulled together. Ken and Daria are your guides on where to go and what questions to ask to build the future you have always dreamed of. This is a book I endorse and will recommend to my own subscribers.

Doug Fabian
President and Editor
Fabian Investment Resources

INTRODUCTION

Personal Finance and the Internet

Over the years on our popular national radio show, we have fielded more than 35,000 personal finance questions from listeners across America—including Hawaii. Although our show specializes in answering a wide variety of questions, one question keeps coming up even after all these years:

> **"How do I start learning about money matters and take control of my personal finances without some salesperson pressuring me to buy something?"**

Although many of our listeners realize that there has never been a better time than *now* to take control, excuses abound. "I'm too busy… There are too many choices… I can't find someone to help me…"

In the past, many investors and potential investors were confused and discouraged by the dazzling array of products and services available from people claiming to be experts—financial planners, insurance salesmen, stockbrokers, and even well-meaning relatives. For many in this cadre of experts, the mantra has been, "Don't worry, I'll take care of your investments. You're too _____ (busy, stupid, confused, and so on)." They were right… Many investors sure have been "taken good care of"—right to the courthouse, or even the poorhouse! For the investor who's willing to commit to a few minutes with this book and the Internet, those days of confusion and frustration are long gone.

Nothing upsets us more than callers who have become convinced that they simply can't understand even the basics of investing. We have two words for you—"baloney" and "Internet"!

("There they go again… the high-tech Dolans." Hardly! We suffered right along with all the other computer novices, learning how to select the best computer for the money and then mastering at least a few of the ways to use the equipment. So don't do a "high-tech" copout on us.)

If we told you that the Internet is a repository of accessible, invaluable, and mostly *free* information that you need to make your life and your family's lives simpler and better, would that get you off the starting line? More than 100 million Americans have access to the Internet, and $1.3 trillion a year will be spent online within the next few years. e-Commerce is the wave of the future. But in our opinion, the incredible usefulness of the information on the Internet has not been fully explored by anyone—until *now*!

There *is* a lot of stuff on the Internet... some good stuff, and a lot of junk! You may already be a burned-out Web surfer, frustrated by Net searches that yield 1,000 different sites or more. Maybe you're just using your computer for email and games, or you've just set up that new computer and you're anxious to get going. "Okay, Dolans, I'm here—*now* what?"

Fair enough. We'll take that challenge. We're very confident that you'll become a convert to the Information Age when you unleash the power of the Internet. In fact, we guarantee it. "*Guarantee?!?* I don't hear that word very much on your show!" You won't hear it when we're talking about investing, but here's why we feel comfortable using that word in this case:

> **We've taken all the work out of cruising the Internet for the kinds of investing/family/personal finance sites that will serve you best, whether you're expecting a new child, financing college for your child, buying a home or a car, or planning for a golden retirement... and many stops in between.**

We know that if we can maximize the results of your first few minutes on the Internet by keeping you from surfing for worthless sites, we'll have you hooked. Think of it... information at your fingertips, 24 hours a day, seven days a week, without a pushy salesperson or a cold call during dinner. (Oops, sorry, we can't guarantee that last one.) The Internet is an almost limitless source of information that will enable you to take control of your financial life, possibly for the first time. Imagine the feeling of power!

Benefit from Our Research

We've scoured thousands of sites to find the most timely and helpful ones. In this book, we won't just list a bunch of sites. We'll give some background information on each subject and show you how to navigate around each site. Try *this* for empowerment—spend a few minutes with this book and the Internet, and you'll know

- As much as—if not more than—your stockbroker about the background information on a particular stock.

- The cost of a car before you enter the dealership to negotiate the best deal.

- Prevailing interest rates before you go to the bank for a mortgage.

- How much different brokerage firms are charging to transact stock and bond trades.

- The best rates for your insurance needs so you can evaluate the different policy options.

- Little-known sources of college funding.

- How to budget so that you can start putting some bucks away for a rainy day.

- How to buy and sell your home online.

- How to update your investment mix as your family's needs change.

- How to get back on a strong credit track.

- Where to find the most comprehensive *free* stock research sites.

- How to plan for your retirement while protecting your assets from Uncle Sam.

… and *much* more!

See where we're headed with this? Never again will you have to depend on what someone else *thinks* you should know! You're in for a pleasant surprise the first time someone asks you, "How did you know that?"

Let's be realistic here… this book won't make you a financial guru. You may still choose to work with a financial professional, but if you're serious enough to commit to 30 minutes a day with us on the Internet, you'll become an informed and empowered investor. You won't be overwhelmed by a salesperson or become victim to the latest "hot" investment scam.

Whether you're an Internet veteran or neophyte, you're in for an incredible experience. The old chestnut "Information is power" has never been truer or timelier, nor has it meant more to you and your family. So clear your head, limber up those fingers, and grab the mouse—let's rock!

PART I

Getting Started

CHAPTER 1

What Is Personal Finance?

You've cracked this book open, so you must have told yourself that personal finance means something to you—even if you're not 100% sure what personal finance is. The very act of going out and buying a book that will help you manage your financial affairs is significant. Why? Because not everyone does it. In fact, far too many people let their personal finances slide, ignoring the basic tools that could enable them to get greater satisfaction and joy out of everyday life. What do we mean by that? Well, personal finance has a way of overlapping with just about every aspect of your life, and managing it—or at a bare minimum, keeping tabs on it—will make life that much better.

Consider your life so far. No matter how old you are or where you are in life, you've spent money. Chances are, you've earned money as well. That's *personal finance*. You've already done it. Like a corporation, you've had net cash inflows and outflows, and you've had a balance sheet. Now, whether you've ever kept track of these inflows and outflows is another question. But if you've tracked things (and we really hope you've at least tried), well, that's *managing your personal finances*. You've done that too. Along the way, you've probably spent some of your money on something big, like a car, a house, or maybe just monthly rent on an apartment. Whatever it is, that's called *deploying your cash*. If you have any cash left over after paying for stuff, you might have bought something fun, like a giant TV or a vacation to Aruba. Or maybe you've bought something practical, like a life insurance policy. If you're in really good shape, you've done both.

What You'll Learn in This Chapter:

▶ The importance of personal finance in your daily life.

▶ The components of personal finance.

▶ The impact of stock markets and financial news on other components of personal finance.

Do you see how managing your money's inflow and outflow can help you enhance your life, making more room for the fun and the practical alike? That's personal finance in action!

People aren't corporations, of course, and you probably don't refer to the money you make as "net cash inflow." That's jargon, and you don't need it in order to manage your money. All you really need is an understanding of the basics and how they all fit together to form your overall personal finance picture.

More Than Meets the Eye

As you might know, there's quite a bit more to personal finance than just keeping track of money coming in and going out. Nothing in life is simple, right? And personal finance, at first glance, can be pretty complicated—if you let it. Indeed, if you don't approach your money matters piece by piece, step by step, you might find yourself swirling amid budgets and bank statements, getting confused and finally getting fed up with the whole thing. Don't let that happen! At that point, you won't manage things as well as you could, and you already know about some of the great things in life that you can get when you *do* manage things well—a college education or a trip to Aruba, not to mention a comfortable retirement.

To help you understand what you're getting into when you start managing your personal finances, let's look at the different components. There's a site on the Internet that shows a sort of cross-section of personal finance. This is *Money* magazine's Web site, which you can reach at *http://www.pathfinder.com/money/*. *Money*, as you might know, is one of a number of magazines specializing in personal finance; due to the potential of the Internet to reach out to people, all of the major financial magazines have developed pretty extensive Web sites in the past couple of years.

Okay, once you have the home page in front of you, we can get started. First, you're staring at a page full of financial news and information. If it all looks "greek" to you, don't worry. Where you want to be is at the very top of *Money*'s home page, above all the topics that are updated daily. Go to the menu bar at the very top of the page. It's a bar running from left to right, beginning with the Home button and followed by a selection of topics.

There… see it? Not too scary, huh? Just a lot of different categories: Markets, News, Investing, Real Estate, Insurance, Autos, Retirement, Taxes, and Tools. If you click on Tools, you'll find help for all the categories.

Money.com, Money magazine's Web site, has lots to offer, from breaking news to planning tools.

This is personal finance reduced to its most basic elements. Each topic here is a piece of the overall picture that you can tackle on its own. Take them one at a time and you won't be overwhelmed. Add them all together at some point, as no doubt you will, and you'll be well on your way to managing the big picture, as complicated as it might seem to be.

Let's discuss a few of these pieces and how they fit together. They'll be covered in much more detail later in this book.

First, the two topics farthest to the left: markets and news. These aren't quite the same as the rest of the categories up there. In fact, they're not things you can manage at all. You certainly can't control what direction the stock market takes (ahhh, if wishes could come true!), and you don't have much of a say in what happens in the day's news, either. But the activity in the world's stock markets and the news coming from corporations, governments, and just about anywhere else can have a big effect on the other topics listed here. If the stock market hits new highs, for example, it could be a pretty nice day over in the retirement area—you know, that topic toward the right end of the menu bar. That's because all the stocks stashed away in a retirement portfolio—hopefully, yours—could be increasing in value. Of course, Uncle Sam is awaiting his cut of the profits you've earned in that sky-rocketing stock market. See how it's all connected?

Bits and Bytes:

Any company that's public, such as General Motors, has to tell the world about its bad news—such as an unexpected problem selling cars—as well as its good news. That's called *disclosure*. Publicly held companies have to file quarterly reports with the Securities & Exchange Commission saying exactly what happened and why.

It's a similar idea with news. If General Motors announces it's having trouble selling cars and trucks, that could send ripples through other parts here on the menu bar. The company might react by adding rebates to its products, making it easier for you to buy. Or GM's stock might shed some of its value. If you've invested in that stock, you might be unhappy; or you might figure that the sales problem in GM showrooms is just temporary and decide to buy more stock in the company while it's cheaper. This activity falls under the investing area.

While we're on the topic, investing is the third item on *Money*'s menu bar. As you've just read, it relates to the buying and selling of stocks, as well as bonds and other types of securities. Simply put, securities represent your ownership in something, usually a corporation (in which case you'd own shares of that company), or your position as a creditor (in which case, as a bondholder, in effect you'd be lending money to a company or government body). Ideally, investments grow—although usually with some risk. In some cases, they can even lose money. But investing is the single best way for you to make your money earn *more* money. It's kind of like planting a seed and watching it grow into a tree that then disperses more seeds you can later plant.

Next on the menu bar is real estate—the practice of buying and selling property, be it your home, a piece of land, or investment property. Real estate is an important part of personal finance. Generally, you can't buy it without having managed your money fairly well, and owning property can contribute significantly to your future financial well-being. It's a form of security in its own right. You get a place to call your own, while hopefully your property grows in value so that by the time you want to sell it, you'll make money. In that sense, real estate is also an investment.

Insurance is a necessary evil in personal finance. After all, who would want to go out and spend money on something you hope you never have to use, such as fire or car collision insurance? But because insurance is so necessary, whether it's for a home, a car, or your life, it's an important part of personal finance. Do it right, and you'll be fully protected against the nasty little surprises that life can bring. Do it wrong, and you'll not only be furious when that flood hits your basement or that tree falls on your car, but you could also suffer a major financial hit.

On to autos. Some people might argue that a car isn't a vital part of anyone's personal finance picture. After all, many people get by perfectly well without ever owning or leasing a car. But let's face it, cars are sufficiently expensive that they usually require financing—that is, borrowing money to buy them. Whenever borrowing money is involved, that's a matter of personal finance.

What's next? Retirement? A-ha!—one of the biggest mysteries of personal finance for many people. It's *so* mysterious because many people don't have a clear grasp of how they're going to do it; they just know they want to. Many people just put it off and figure it's out there somewhere, waiting for them when they turn 65. But planning for your retirement can eliminate most of the mystery and ensure that those dreams of round-the-world cruises or golf course nirvana can come true.

Finally, taxes. You know what they say: The only sure things in life are death and taxes. And in personal finance, taxes are certainly a constant presence. Invest in some stock, do well and make money, and what do you get? Taxes. See that car? Like it? Think *that's* the price? Not so fast. You have to pay taxes. You get the picture. Managing your personal finances without considering taxes is like driving a car without watching traffic lights: Sooner or later, you'll crash.

Now you've seen the basics of personal finance. There's more that *Money* isn't telling you about in this simple menu bar, but don't worry—you've got this book. And you have the Internet, a tremendous resource for anyone who wants to better manage his or her personal finances. The following chapters are going to walk you through the essential elements of personal finance and show you how the Internet can be an increasingly effective tool for managing your money.

So fire up that computer and rev up that Web browser! Let's go!

On Your Way

You're an expert now, right? Okay, maybe not. But at least you're familiar with what personal finance means, and you're ready to learn about all of its many little details, particularly how you can use the Internet to help. By now you've learned the following:

- Even if you don't know it, you've already been dealing with personal finance issues just by earning and spending money.

- Managing your personal finances will make it a lot easier to get the things you want from life, such as vacations, a college education for you or your kids, and a comfortable retirement.

- It's best to understand all aspects of personal finance, not just those that might interest you, because no two elements in personal finance are truly isolated from one another. For instance, things that happen with your taxes can have a significant effect on what happens in your retirement portfolio.

CHAPTER 2

How Can I Use the Internet for Personal Finance?

For years, some people did just fine managing their money without having the Internet around to make things easier. They used money-management software on their home computers. Before that, in the dark ages of technology, they employed calculators and adding machines to churn out numbers. And before that, of course, there was good old pencil, paper, a little brainpower, and plenty of erasers.

But now that we have the Internet in its full "dot-com" glory, we've entered a whole new realm of personal finance management. The Internet and personal finance are made for each other. With its interactive capabilities, tons and tons of information, ability to offer material for downloading directly onto your home computer's hard drive, and sense of community, the Internet is a natural tool for anyone seeking to make the most of his or her money. You can calculate possible financial moves long before you actually intend to do anything about them. You can access reams and reams of financial news, historical data (that is, data from years past that you can use to help predict what might happen with a stock or some other investment), and background information on financial topics. You can do your own research—much of it for free—and thus avoid paying a high-priced professional, such as a broker, accountant, or attorney, to do it for you. You can get tax forms without budging from your seat. And of course, you can "talk" to thousands of people just like you all over the world: people with questions and answers on the same topics you're wondering about, people with ideas about things

What You'll Learn in This Chapter:

▶ What personal finance portals are and how best to use them.

▶ How community sites work and how they can help you.

▶ How educational Web sites can teach you about personal finance.

▶ What transaction-oriented financial Web sites do.

▶ How vendor-run financial sites work.

▶ How calculators work.

you've considered, and—who knows?—maybe even insomniacs who just want to chat about money matters at 2 a.m. while they eat a midnight snack at their kitchen table.

For more information on using historical financial data to predict investment activity, see Chapter 8, "Investing Online—Growing Your Nest Egg."

Because the Internet is such a good fit with all things financial, providers of financial information have colonized it to an enormous extent. There are thousands and thousands of financial Web sites, and more debut every day. Financial transactions on the Web, such as stock trading and banking, are among the most common uses of the Internet as a whole. Indeed, many people only know the Internet as a means of conducting their personal financial business.

But where do you begin? As you probably know, for all the Internet's splendid usefulness, it can be a bewildering mess of "World Wide Web" this and "dot-com" that, with a dizzying array of more than 1 billion sites. Combine that with uncertainty about personal finance, which can be painfully confusing, and you could have quite an unnerving mess on your hands.

Relax. That's why you're reading this book. You just need to take it one step at a time. This chapter will go over the basic types of Web sites that offer particular kinds of personal finance information. You'll see these kinds of sites over and over and over again in this book, and you'll quickly learn to recognize them as soon as you see them loading onto your computer screen.

With that, let's get started!

Personal Finance Portals

A *portal* is a door, a passage, or a conduit from one side of something to another. In Internet lingo, a portal is a comprehensive, generalized Web site that acts as a door to information that you select at will. Because personal finance has spread to so many corners of the Internet, it's not surprising that there are dozens of portals specializing in this area. Media, such as magazines and TV networks, run many of them (like *Money* magazine's site, which you checked out briefly in Chapter 1), and software companies, such as Microsoft or Intuit, run others.

You need to understand a couple of things right from the beginning. These portals aren't run for charity. As useful as they are (and they can indeed be extremely useful), many are laden with ads and run by companies that would very much like you to buy their magazines, watch their TV channels, use their software, and do whatever else makes them some money now or later. But that should not dissuade you from using these personal finance portals. You'd be foolish not to go to SmartMoney's site or Microsoft's financial site just because they might profit from your visit. Very few other sites can offer the kind of comprehensive content these sites can—content that is fresh just about 365 days a year and run by smart, professional people handpicked for their knowledge in this area.

Just don't lose your head if you see a little blurb in the corner of a site saying, "Subscribe to our magazine." Take it with a grain of salt. All the portals discussed here are free, as are many of the personal finance sites, so realize that you're getting an enormous wealth of information for nothing. You can probably ignore the occasional "buy this" in exchange for the info, right? Besides, none of the good personal finance portals are pushy. Instead, they come across as giant repositories of news and information that happen to be branded like a product, such as Quicken, Intuit's personal finance portal and software.

How to Use Portals

The best way to use a portal is to find one you like and bookmark it on your Web browser. Why? Because a portal is a gateway to future research and activities you'll do on the Internet, and you're sure to go back regularly to your portal as a starting point for personal finance tasks. All portals have links to other sites, so you might start out at *Money*'s portal for some basic info on car insurance and then, armed with ideas on the subject, link from there to some car insurance providers' sites. The next day, you might want data on IRAs, so you start out at *Money*'s site again and zoom to various IRA sites you find on the portal. Get the idea? Portals are starting points.

Let's visit a portal and get a quick idea of what's available there. Try Microsoft's massive MSN MoneyCentral site at *http://moneycentral.msn.com/home.asp* as an example. Pull up the home page. Like many personal finance portals, it has information on all those different topics discussed in Chapter 1. To the left is a menu of personal finance topics, quite similar to the *Money* magazine menu bar. There are some differences—family and college, for example, and nothing on autos—but the idea is exactly the same.

MoneyCentral's Portal is a good place to start for less savvy Web surfers.

On the right is the content that's updated daily: news, announcements, and something called Today's Best, a feature chosen by the MSN editors. As you know, news can have an enormous impact on your finances, so almost every financial portal places it front and center, usually with updates throughout the business day.

Below the menu, on the left, are numbers showing the stock market's performance, another standby of any financial portal (and indeed, a hallmark of many financial Web sites these days). These numbers are also updated frequently—in some cases, they're almost exactly in real-time and thus are updated almost constantly. For anyone following investments or just eager to know what the stock market is doing on any given day at any given time, these numbers are key.

Move back up to the top of the page and look above the menu on the left. See the blank text box marked Quotes & Research? That's another hallmark of a personal finance portal (and again, it's found on many other less comprehensive sites as well). It's a tool you can use to find out the latest price of a given stock or mutual fund. You simply key in the ticker symbol—a series of letters that represents a particular stock or fund—and you get the price that the security is trading at on the stock exchange that day (or, if you're doing it on the weekend, what price it closed at the previous Friday). Usually, quotes are delayed by 20 minutes or so on many Web sites, so the price you see is just a sense of how things are going for that particular stock or fund at that particular time.

Searching on a Topic

Are you starting to see how much you can do on one portal? There's more. This is just the home page. Move back down below the menu, on the left. You'll see another blank text box, labeled Search MoneyCentral, into which you can type keywords. This kind of feature, present on just about any portal, is particularly useful. Suppose you run across MSN's site in a moment of desperation, dying to get some information on private mortgage insurance. You're so rattled after a frustrating morning of mortgage hell that you don't even think to look at the subjects in the menu bar, and you just want to go straight to information on this topic without wading through general info on mortgages. Go ahead—do it.

1. Type "private mortgage insurance" in the Search MoneyCentral text box.

▼ **Try It Yourself**

2. Click Go. See? In this case, you get more than 10 pages on which the site has covered private mortgage insurance.

3. Choose the particular page you want. Now you're in business, dealing with the subject you want rather than a general treatise on mortgages.

▲

Almost all portals maintain huge repositories or archives of past news, articles, and information on a given topic, so you'll usually be able to find what you want by using their Search features.

Community Sites

Now let's look at sites that are built around a community, or a sense of community. They may be run by a company with a profit motive (as the portals are), by a person with an interest in a particular topic, or by an association or non-profit organization that wants to be sure people are aware of a given topic or have a chance to discuss it. In any case, community sites generally put a strong emphasis on sharing and discussing ideas, whether it's by message boards, chat rooms, or newsgroups. You'll find some of these elements in other sites—for instance, many portals have message boards—but a community site's *main* function is to provide a forum for exchanging ideas and tips on a particular topic.

One example is *http://www.401kafe.com*, which bills itself as "the community resource for 401(k) participants." A 401(k), as you might know, is a type of retirement savings plan. This site, which is run by a group called the 401(k) Forum, is marked by a heavy emphasis on message boards and on sharing the latest news on 401(k) plans. It acts as a virtual club that's open to anyone with something to learn, share, or discuss about 401(k) plans.

At the 401Kafe, you can stay informed on all aspects of your 401(k).

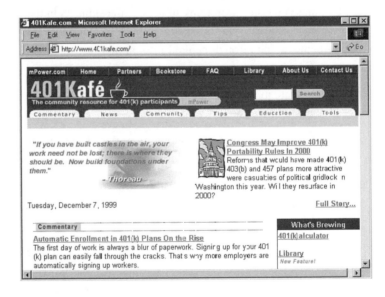

Bits and Bytes:

Did you know that you'll be penalized for withdrawing from your 401(k) plan before you're age 59 1/2? The rap: you pay an extra 10% in tax penalties, and the total amount withdrawn is taxable. The same is true of other retirement plans, such as traditional IRAs, SEPs, 403(B)s, and Keogh plans.

"University Sites"

Ready to hit the books? Many financial Web sites have gone to great lengths to offer "university sites"—so named because

almost all of them use a college gimmick, such as referring to
their classes as Investing 101, Mortgages 101, and so on. A lot of
them even come right out and call themselves universities. You
won't get a degree by using them, of course, but you will get a
nice primer on the basics of personal finance, particularly
investing.

Investing lends itself so well to these university sites because it's
among the most complicated areas of personal finance. There are
so many nuances and aspects of investing that entire Web
"schools" have sprung up to educate people like you on the finer
points of stock-picking, reading annual reports, and so on.

But whether they're for investing specifically or personal finance
in general, online university sites are a category that warrants
some exploration. They're popping up all over the place, usually
as part of a larger site devoted to finance. You know you've hit
one when you see the "101" stuff or anything else related to
classes and tutorials. But we're not knocking them. These
"courses" are free and can be very useful as you educate yourself
on personal finance.

Let's check out a couple of these sites. First, try SmartMoney
University, one of the first of the university sites to come along.
It's at *http://www.university.smartmoney.com*. As you scroll down
the page, you'll see classes organized as neatly as if this were a
college catalogue. You need to "register" for classes here, but it's
completely free. When you click on the link inviting you to register, you get information on how the university works, certain
classes you probably want to take first, and so on. It's not that different from a real college—except that it's online, it doesn't give
you any credit, and it's free. Oh yeah, and no tests!

Now let's look at Fool's School, which is at
http://www.fool.com/school.htm. Like SmartMoney University,
this "school" offers a range of courses starting with the most
basic and progressing up from there. You're invited to read
"lessons" based on what other participants have asked before.
However, unlike SmartMoney University, Fool's School is oriented more toward investing than general personal finance.

SmartMoney University offers brief online courses that might help you manage your personal finances better.

Not all learning sites are set up quite like universities, but they fall into the category nonetheless. One site that goes to particularly strenuous lengths not to use unfamiliar jargon and other insider stuff that could turn off finance novices is Green, which you'll find at *http://www.greenmagazine.com*. This site is aimed at young and inexperienced people who are just entering the world of personal finance, so it's trying hard to relate to its users in their language. Its educational features have names like How to Do Stuff and What the Hell's a... (which explains what a bond is, for instance). Many other sites will just presume that if you're there, you already know what bonds are or how stocks work. This site doesn't. The information is every bit as sophisticated as it is at other sites, but it begins at ground zero and works its way up from there.

Back to School

Another interesting learning site is *http://www.learn2.com/*. As you first glance at this site's home page, you might wonder what on earth it has to do with personal finance. You might see articles titled Learn to Repair a Doorknob or Learn to Treat a Dog Bite. Huh? But that's the beauty of this site! It's made up of nothing but tutorials on an incredibly wide range of subjects. And over on the left, the tutorials are listed by topic. Sure enough, there are a whole bunch under Business and Money. There, you'll find everything from Learn to Read the Stock Market Pages to Learn to Conduct Business on the Web. Each tutorial is laid out in the most fundamental fashion imaginable, telling you the materials you'll need before starting and how long it will take to walk through the course. They're not unlike those fun cooking shows where the chefs start out with all the ingredients laid out on the counter. Sprinkled amid the full-length tutorials are Learnlets, little snippets of other helpful information.

Bottom line? This is a great site if you've got some time on your hands and feel like walking through something slowly. And who knows? You might wind up a doorknob-repair expert at the same time.

Transaction Sites

Another kind of financial Web site is one that actually lets you perform financial transactions. Some of these sites are also portals, or at least *seem* to be portals. But their primary function is to conduct financial business, such as banking or investing. No doubt you've heard of the revolution going on in the brokerage industry, in which anyone can buy and sell stock for a fraction of what it used to cost at a full-service firm. Stock trades that used to cost well over $100 in commissions just a few years ago are now routinely done for less than $10 on some Internet brokerage sites. One of the best-known online brokerages, E*Trade, is located at *http://www.etrade.com.*

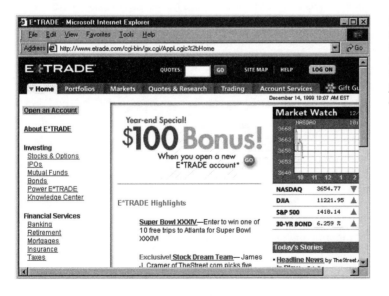

E*Trade's site offers lots of information, but remember that they really want you to trade stocks there.

**For more informa-
tion on paying bills
online,** see Chapter
4, "Banking
Online—Managing
Your Money over
the Internet," and
Chapter 8.

Likewise, millions of people are now paying bills online instead
of writing out checks, stuffing envelopes, and searching for
stamps. One important thing to know: Unlike so much of the
Internet, generally these are not free sites. Someone has to make
money from these transactions, so you will pay a commission or
fee to trade stocks online or do banking transactions (such as paying those bills). But you'll pay far less than you would doing the
same transactions the old-fashioned way, at least for stock trades.
Transaction-oriented sites also contain tons of news, analysis,
research, and commentary to help you make transactions.
Sometimes this information is free whether you have an account
with that site or not.

Calculator Crazy

Okay, so you know that the Internet and personal finance are a
match made in heaven. But the truest show of affection between
the two parties is the amazing proliferation of calculators on Web
sites far and wide. Calculators? As in… little solar-powered giz-
mos with buttons? Well, not really. They do far more than add,
subtract, and figure out square roots. They're interactive tools
found on Web sites that are set up around particular topics—such
as mortgages or car leases. You enter information into them, such
as your income, debt, and so on. The calculators then calculate
how much house you can buy, for instance, or how much you can
afford to spend on your monthly car payment.

Calculators are ubiquitous on the Internet these days, showing up
in many of the portals, many specific sites, and tons of vendors'
sites. And why not? Everyone likes an interactive tool, and they're
easy to use. Online vendors figure that if you spend time using
their calculator, you might stick around long enough to consider
their mortgage, car loan, or whatever else they sell.

There are even Web sites set up mainly for calculators. One of
them is FinancCenter.com's ClickCalcs. Find the home page at
http://www.financenter.com and click on ClickCalcs at the bottom,
in the blue navigation bar. You'll find different areas of personal
finance—autos, insurance, home, and so on—and for each one
there's a scroll bar with a long list of calculators, categorized as
questions. For example, are you pondering a car purchase and
wondering "How much should depreciation cost me?" or "Should

I lease or purchase?" Presto! There's a calculator for each of those questions, and many more. One nifty feature: These calculators go a step beyond mere math by explaining and graphically illustrating their findings. Each calculator comes with five tabs, labeled Inputs, Results, Graphs, Explanations, and Deals. After you find the results, you just click on a tab for the expanded information. The Deals tab is hyperlinked to vendor Web sites that can hook you up with car loans, mortgages, and so on.

One caveat, however: A calculator's answers should never be taken literally. If some mortgage calculator tells you that a $500,000 home will be no problem, don't go out the next day and start driving around Hilltop Estates looking for a stone mansion. You can't base real-life financial decisions on what a Web site's calculator tells you, no matter how believable it sounds. All Internet calculators are intended to be tools, helpers, or enablers—they're supposed to *guide* you to your financial decisions, not make them for you.

Vendor Sites

Finally, there are financial vendor sites. They're not the same as transaction sites, although often you can interact with them by asking for more information on a particular product or service. But understand that these sites are run by large companies that sell financial services, such as insurance and mutual funds. You might find a lot of useful information on such a site, but there's usually going to be a sales pitch lurking around the corner—some of them not too subtle. The vendors think these sites are great image-builders, so they slap those Web addresses onto all their magazine ads and TV commercials in the hope that you'll go there one afternoon and find out all about their products, their company's history, and so on. We're not necessarily opposed to these sites. Some of them can be sort of fun, and many of them contain valuable information and links (not to mention useful things like stock quotes and calculators), but their main purpose is to sell you something.

For instance, MetLife's fun little Life Advice Center, at *http://www.metlife.com*, covers topics such as sending your kids to camp (including a handy little checklist of what they should

bring) and talking to your parents about retirement homes. That's
MetLife trying to be helpful in the hopes that you'll buy some
insurance if you need it. Visit vendor sites at your own risk—you
might buy something you don't need or want.

On Your Way

Now you know that the Internet is positively packed with information on personal finance. But before you move on and learn
exactly how to use this information, let's review some of the
things discussed in this chapter:

- Financial portals are giant, comprehensive sites that contain a
  great deal of relevant personal finance information, links to
  other sites, and interactive tools. You should bookmark them
  for future reference.

- Community sites can be a good way to exchange ideas with
  other people who share your interest in a given area of personal finance.

- So-called university sites act like virtual schools on the
  Internet, abounding with classes, courses, and the other trap-
  pings of an educational institution. They offer good primers
  on finance basics.

- People use the Internet to conduct financial transactions at
  lower cost on specialized sites set up for this purpose, such as
  online brokerages and banks.

- Many financial service vendors have set up Web sites to pol-
  ish their image among consumers. Much of the information
  on these sites can be found elsewhere.

PART II

Setting Up a Good Strategy

CHAPTER 3

Budgeting—Planning for Today and the Future

Now you're ready to sit down and use the Internet. As you know by now, you're in the right place. There are Web sites for just about every aspect of personal finance. So, mouse in hand, fingers poised above your computer keyboard, maybe a cup of steaming coffee within reach... where should you start? Well, it might make the most sense to start at the very beginning—with a *budget*. It all starts there.

Budgeting makes the rest of your personal financial picture fall into place a little more neatly. For example, it's easier to decide how much to start setting aside in a brokerage account when you know how much you need for essential expenses every month. You really can't start to plan for the future until you have a good handle on where things stand right now. Once you do, you can figure out a game plan—maybe it's all about paying off some debt, or maybe it's more about starting to invest your money. You won't know where to go until your budget is in place. Think of it as a roadmap for the rest of your financial forays.

Before we get started on the Web sites that can help you create a budget—and more importantly, stick to it—let's talk about what goes into one. Whether you've been budgeting for years or this is the first time you've ever said the "b" word, it helps to first walk through the fundamental steps .

Simply put, a budget indicates how much money you bring in on a regular basis and how much you spend—what comes in and what goes out. You can do a budget on an annual, quarterly, monthly, weekly, or even daily basis. When it comes to personal finances, most people look at budgets on a monthly basis because

What You'll Learn in This Chapter:

▶ What a budget is and how to create one.

▶ What your net worth means to your budget.

▶ How to use specialized budget calculators on the Internet.

▶ How your current budget affects your future ability to save money.

▶ Where to find discussion groups about budgets.

▶ How home budgeting software can interface with the Internet.

so many regular expenses—mortgages, utility payments, car loans—are billed month to month. But if you're finding too much month left at the end of your paycheck, you might want to start out by doing a weekly budget. The shorter time frame might make it easier to track easy-to-overlook expenses that are adding up regularly, such as $3-$5 for lunches here and there. It might seem inconsequential, but it could wind up costing you $15-$25 a week.

Bits and Bytes:
Don't forget to assign a line for savings in your fixed expenses. Saving can be a difficult habit to get into. It's so easy to blow it off when you'd rather spend the day at the mall or order that pizza. But if you think of it as a set payment to yourself every month, before you know it you'll be well on your way to a tidy nest egg. Even if you just start with $10 a week, less than the cost of that pizza, you'll come out ahead.

To create a budget, start by looking at your income—your monthly take-home pay, plus any other income you receive. This is what you're bringing in every month, after taxes. Then look at your monthly fixed expenses—"fixed" meaning they stay the same, month after month. This could include rent, a mortgage payment, a commuter pass, or a car payment. You should also include the monthly portion of any quarterly payments, such as insurance payments. Then list your flexible expenses, which can vary from month to month: clothing, food, entertainment, etc. Now look for problem areas. If you're short every month, you could cut down in a flexible area, such as entertainment. Or you could set a goal to eliminate a fixed expense (such as a pesky credit card bill) within six months by shifting more to that payment from one of your flexible expenses. See how easy it is to get the big picture when everything is written out?

You can build upon the same basic budget formula even when you have more complicated scenarios, including things like dual incomes, interest and tax payments, automatic savings plans, and other factors that affect a budget.

Budget Starting Points on the Web

Now that you're getting the idea, let's try visiting some sites that can help with setting up your budget. Break the ice by trying a budget game run by the American Bankers Association, a trade group for banks. Naturally, banks are eager for you to take budgeting seriously, hoping that some of that dough will start flowing into their savings accounts, and that's okay. Whether you open an account or stuff your money under your mattress (though we certainly hope you come up with a better plan than *that),* you can still play the ABA's fun little online budget game. Just go to *http://www.aba.com/aba/ConsumerConnection/CNC_games.htm.* This is part of the ABA's Consumer Connection portion of its Web site, and the game is sponsored by the ABA Education Foundation.

The game uses Shockwave, a downloadable computer program that will let you interact with the Web site's host computer. It takes a few moments to load, faster or slower depending on how fast your own computer is. Once it starts, it's very much like using a CD-ROM, with colorful graphics and full-motion video. You meet "Penny Banks," an economist in Washington, who walks you through what a budget is and why you need one. Penny is heavy on the humor—which is helpful when it comes to budgeting. The ABA's budget game certainly isn't a serious tool for setting up a budget, but if nothing else it's a fun few minutes.

Had your laughs? Now you're ready for some real work. Whether you're firmly in the black or you're showing a tinge of red ink, knowing where you stand will put you on the path to a new budget. Let's try a calculator that can help you figure out your net worth. This net worth calculator resides on *SmartMoney* magazine's SmartMoney Interactive at *http://www.smartmoney.com/ac/estate/index.cfm?story=networth.* All you have to do here is follow the directions and type in your information: your assets, such as any property you own, and your liabilities, such as debts. It's as simple as that.

For more information on portals, see Chapter 2, "How Can I Use the Internet for Personal Finance?"

Knowing your net worth is a way to gauge progress.

For more information on lowering your insurance premium to save money, see Chapter 6, "Insurance—Finding the Best Policy Online."

For more information on wealth preservation, see Chapter 8, "Investing Online—Growing Your Nest Egg" and Chapter 13, "Wills and Estate Planning—Taking Care of Your Heirs."

At the very least, this calculator is an eye opener in a very simple format. That number at the bottom of your page says a lot about how you might want to start running your finances. If you have a negative net worth—that is, you owe more than you own—you should start thinking about whittling down your debt. If you have a positive net worth, pat yourself on the back! You're ahead of the game. Now you can start thinking about wealth accumulation, such as investments and savings. If you have a higher net worth, you might look into wealth preservation, such as a trust to protect your assets for your heirs.

Specialized Budget Calculators

Remember how calculators are taking over the Internet in not-so-subtle ways? Well, they're out in force when it comes to budgeting. They can really help you figure out how changing your budget now can help you set aside savings for the future, which is something your regular old monthly budget probably didn't do.

Let's revisit FinanCenter's nifty calculators, which are so good at breaking down all that information so that you can understand it. Go to *http://www.financenter.com/budgeting.html.*

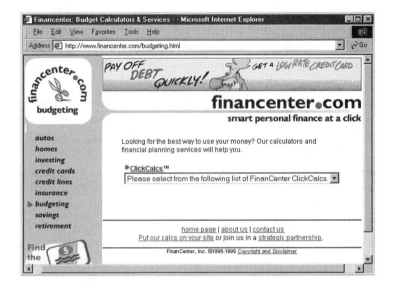

1. On this page, you'll see a whole selection of specialized budget calculators. Let's try "How Much Am I Spending?" It's the second one from the top.

2. You're looking at two columns, current spending and desired spending, for just about every element of a household budget, ranging from home payments and maintenance to utilities, clothing, entertainment, even alimony. Enter your own information. At the bottom, enter your monthly after-tax income, the rate of return you get on your savings, and your state and federal tax rates. Then click "results."

3. You get a table depicting how much you could save if you used your new budget and, based on the rate of return you entered on the first page, how much you'd have after 10 years of using this budget.

▼ **Try It Yourself**

4. Now look at some of the other information here, based on the data you just entered. If you go to the graphs tab at the top, you get a graph showing two lines: yellow for your current situation and blue for the desired situation. If numbers mean nothing to you, this will help a lot. It's a clear depiction of how your money will grow if you change your spending habits.

5. Not sure what it all means? Click on the explanation tab. There it is, short and sweet: "This calculator illustrates the dramatic effects which small reductions in spending can have on long-term investments and, especially, the funds you will have available at retirement."

Now, keep in mind that in a few years your budget could significantly change from what it is now. If you're single now, you might get married, have kids, and thus increase your expenses. Or if you're putting kids through college now, you'll watch them leave the nest and thus decrease your expenses. Plus, your income will almost certainly change. So don't panic if you don't like what you see. As with many Web calculator results, it's just a guideline. But based on your current situation, it's a pretty good way to see the growth potential of the money you're currently wasting each month.

For more information on the impact of credit cards on personal finance, see Chapter 5, "Credit and Debt—Taking Care of Your Liabilities Using the Internet."

Another good budget calculator further down that list is "What Will It Take to Pay Off My Balance?" (Click Budgeting, the menu at the left, to get back to the calculator page.) If you've ever doubted the nasty dent that credit cards can make in your personal finances, this will show you in cold, hard numbers. Brace yourself—it can get ugly. In just a few keystrokes, you can find out how long you'll be in debt, based on the amount you currently owe to each debtor, future monthly charges and payments, any annual fees and interest rates, and future rate changes. It's enough to make you whip out the scissors and starting cutting up those cards on the spot. Whether you do or not, it's a good way to see how credit cards affect your budget, which will allow you to do more long-range planning.

Information Is Power

Raw numbers are one thing, but information is another. All the calculators in the world won't necessarily tell you how to get the most out of your budget and how to save more. That's why you might want to visit a more community-oriented site.

Let's try *Family Money* magazine's site at *http://www. familymoney.com*, which has some tools for budgeting and discussion groups on the topic. At the home page, you'll see the Budgeting and Borrowing area over on the menu bar at the left, under Family Finances. Click on that to get a list of articles related to budgeting topics. Some of it is fairly generic information. Naturally, your own situation will be unique, but you can blend the information about your own budget situation that you gained from the calculators with the advice and tips in these articles. And in the *Your Take* section at the top of *Family Money*'s site, you can find discussion groups where you can pose budgeting questions.

Discussion groups offer you the opportunity to pose questions that are specific to your needs.

Another good way to blend your own home budget information with resources on the Internet is to use software specially designed for tracking all those inflows and outflows, and then link some of that data to the software vendor's Web site. One of the most popular of these home budgeting programs is Quicken, which is made by Intuit. Quicken is certainly big in homes—millions of people use it to log in their everyday expenses and reconcile their books every month—but it's also big on the Internet as one of the portal sites discussed in Chapter 2. Join the two and you've got quite a potent combination.

For example, the Quicken 2000 edition gives users one-click access to the QuickAnswers calculators on its Web site, *http://www.quicken.com.* You can use these calculators to test out various options before committing to buying a house, car, or other major item. These calculators are "one size fits all," so you should take your own personal situation into consideration when you look at QuickAnswers' results. And because you can use these calculators simultaneously as you balance your books at home, they can be very useful in determining if you can *really* afford that new car. You can also take information from the Internet and put it into your Quicken software at home, downloading information such as stock and mutual fund quotes directly from Quicken's site. Then compare how various investments perform.

On Your Way

You've started to make some headway with your personal finances by learning how to tackle a budget. With any luck, it won't be too hard to get your basic financial picture assembled and start planning for the future. By now you have learned the following:

- Budgets are composed of income, fixed expenses, and flexible expenses—elements that can point you toward a variety of options.

- If you have a negative net worth, you need to start coming up with ways to cut down some of your debt and expenses. If you have a positive net worth, you're in good shape but ought to think of ways to preserve that wealth and start growing your money.

- Little changes in your spending habits now can have big effects on how much money you can save in the future, once you factor in interest rates on your savings.

- You can use calculators to make some of these projections.

- Home-based software and online resources can make a powerful combination.

CHAPTER 4

Banking Online— Managing Your Money over the Internet

Banking has never been anyone's favorite activity—those long lines snaking through those velvet ropes, poring over monthly statements that defy logic, or wading your way through interminable layers of voice mail just to get a human customer service rep on the phone. So combining the Internet's interactive components and banking's more mundane aspects (such as checking your account balances, writing checks, and so forth) seems like a natural. Who wouldn't like to bank from their home office at 3 a.m., cuddled in a bathrobe?

It's no wonder that just about every mid-sized and large bank in the country has developed a presence on the Web. Banks were among the first businesses to see the vast potential of the Internet and started commercializing it more than five years ago, which was light years ahead of other kinds of companies. So where has their head start gotten them? Actually, not as far as you'd think. No matter how sophisticated the Internet gets, you still can't open a little door on your computer and pull out a few twenties for this week's grocery shopping. Regardless of the types of transactions that banks make available to their Internet customers, they still can't replace some transactions, such as cash withdrawals and immediate check deposits. (At least not yet!) So don't expect your burgeoning Internet bank relationship to mean you never have to set foot in a bank branch again.

This chapter will cover the many banking activities that you can do fairly efficiently over the Internet. It turns out that you can

What You'll Learn in This Chapter:

► The kinds of banking transactions you can conduct via the Internet.

► How to review and compare online banks.

► How to pay your bills online.

► How to search for the best interest rates for different banking products.

conduct many transactions. You can comparison-shop between banks for different interest rates on loans and other products. And you can pay bills—we've all got those, and plenty of them.

What It Means to Access Your Bank Online

There are literally thousands of banks in this country—in fact, more than in any other country in the world. There are tiny banks that just serve one or two communities (they're actually called "community banks"), regional banks that may serve an entire section of the country, and enormous super-regional banks with networks of branches that may stretch from coast to coast. There are also "money center" banks that are based here in the United States and serve many retail customers, but that also operate in foreign countries and do a lot of business lending money to big corporations and other banks. Generally, the different kinds of banks break down by size: community banks are small, regionals are big, super-regionals are very large, and money centers tend to be gigantic.

So what does this mean to you and your yen to bank online? Actually, very little. All you need to know is that on the Internet, bank size doesn't matter too much. A small bank can offer myriad online services. On the other hand, your big super-regional bank that runs branches from Maine to Florida and everywhere in between might not be doing much at all on the Internet. Almost all banks have a presence online, but many of those "presences" are actually just fancy Web sites designed to impress you and ultimately sell you on their services… which you have to conduct the old-fashioned way, in person or perhaps over the phone. In reality, only about 450 banks are set up to conduct true online banking transactions. That sounds like a lot, but it's just a fraction of all the thousands of banks in the country. Granted, that number is growing all the time, but be prepared to find out that your bank, or the one down the street, isn't equipped to conduct many (or any) online transactions at this time.

Disappointed? Don't be—as you'll find out later in this chapter, the beauty of online banking is that you don't need to be anywhere near the bank itself. It comes to you via your modem. You can transfer your account to a far-away bank that does permit online transactions and wind up feeling quite satisfied.

But for now, let's look at some of the transactions and services a typical bank puts online. Open your browser to the Bank of America's home page at *http://www.bankofamerica.com*. This is a super-regional bank if ever there was one. It practically owned the West Coast before it merged with East Coast super-regional NationsBank, and now it's perhaps the closest thing we have to a nationwide bank.

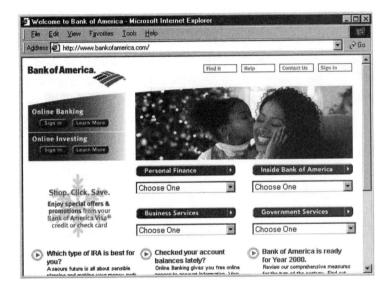

As with most online banks, you can do more than check your account balance at Bank America's Web site.

In the middle of the page is some basic background information on the bank and its services. Nothing too unusual there. But over on the left are the online banking and online investing entrance areas, where you'd sign in if you had an online account with this bank. You don't (well, we're going to presume you don't yet), so click on the Learn More button. After selecting your state (and in some cases, your types of service), Bank of America explains what you can do online: access your accounts to check balances and view previous transactions, transfer money between different accounts, and make specific requests, such as checkbook refills. These are pretty typical online banking transactions. They don't cover every aspect of your banking relationship, but they do cover many basic banking needs.

For more informa-
tion on using
account nicknames,
see Chapter 8,
"Investing Online—
Growing Your Nest
Egg."

Now go over to the left and click the blue bar marked Begin
Demo. You're going to see firsthand what an online banking
account looks like. Start walking through the demo as instructed.
Your first stop is a sample account statement. Looks a little like a
regular old paper statement, doesn't it? Except it's more colorful,
and there's a column heading titled Account Nickname.
Nicknames are frequently used in online banking to make it easier
to keep track of different accounts via your computer—it's a lot
easier to type in a nickname than 10 or so numbers. For example,
you could call your savings account "Nest Egg," or something
personal, like "Joe's Dough." Cute, huh?

Scroll down the list on the left to check out what the various
online banking screens look like. For example, the Transaction
History screen shows all your ATM, debit, and check transactions
much as a traditional paper statement does—except, of course,
that you can see this screen anytime, not just once a month when
your statement arrives in the mail. (That's great for those of you
who aren't such experts at the art of balancing your checkbooks!)
You can also search and sift through this list of transactions by
the type of transaction or the amount—useful for tracking down a
certain debit purchase, for example.

Spend some time clicking on the different account services in that
list on the left. Many of the services are identical to those you'd
find at any bank, in person or over the phone. The difference, of
course, is in the degree to which you interact with your account.
You get the idea. There's a great deal of flexibility to be gained
by banking online.

This is just one example of a bank's online services. Naturally,
each bank's site is different. If you like the idea of doing these
kinds of things over the Internet, check first to see if your bank
offers such online services or merely promotes itself via a Web
site. If your bank is *truly* online, get familiar with how its site and
services are set up. Ideally, it will have a demo feature like the
Bank of America site. Click around in the site and get a feel for it.
Is it easy to navigate? Look for features such as a site map, a FAQ
(frequently asked questions) section, and a technical service area.
And consider hitching up with a bank that has its own network of
branches and ATMs for those things that you can't do online

easily (or at all), such as withdrawing cash or making deposits. Internet-only banks are popping up all over the Net, but these virtual institutions require you to mail in your deposits—as in *snail mail*—and must coordinate with other banks for use of their ATMs, which could cost you more.

Checking Out Online Banks

If you do want to venture into the new, mostly uncharted territory of Internet-only banks, you'll need a guide. Not all Internet-only banking institutions are equal, and you certainly don't want to find out the hard way. You don't want to set up an account only to pull your hair out a month later, when you're stuck navigating some goofy bank Web site that seemed clear when you first saw it but now makes absolutely no sense whatsoever. A good way to find out what's hot and what's not in this fast-changing, fast-moving area is to visit a site that rates this new breed of bank.

Try the Gomez Advisors online banking scorecard at *http://www.gomezadvisors.com.* This site, an independent, consumer-oriented outgrowth of a research and consulting firm that studies electronic commerce, features ratings of everything from online insurance agents to auctions. It's particularly good with banks.

Gomez Advisors gives you consumer ratings on all sorts of e-activities, from banking to travel.

At Gomez Advisors, online banks are rated according to various criteria, and you can see how two or more banks that you might be particularly interested in stack up against each other. The site also has consumer reviews so you can check out what everyday Joes and Janes have to say about a given online bank. You won't see every bank that offers services online. The ratings are limited to Internet-only banks and a handful of their closest relatives: units set up by traditional banks to operate as Internet-focused institutions.

Try It Yourself ▼

1. From the Gomez Advisors home page, go over to the left and click on Banks.

2. Okay, you're at the Gomez "banks central." All of its Internet bank information is at your fingertips. Let's say you want to view the firm's entire Internet bank ratings. Under the very first heading, Which Is the Best Online Bank?, you'll see an invitation to view the Internet banker scorecard by category. Click on Overall Score.

3. You're looking at the Top 20 among the online banks that have been surveyed by Gomez—78 at press time—ranked by their scores. If you want to see all 78 banks, you can click on View All Firms at the bottom of the list.

4. Find out more about how these scores were created by going below the list and clicking on Read About the Bank Scorecard Methodology. You'll get quite a detailed explanation of how Gomez ranks these organizations. When you're finished reading it, click back to the scorecard.

5. Now compare two banks. Over on the right you see two drop-down lists, each labeled Select a Bank, along with a blue button labeled Compare just below them. Scroll down each list and choose a bank. Click Compare.

6. There you have it—two banks pitted against each other, category by category, along with links to their "firm profiles," detailed write-ups from Gomez telling you more about the banks.

▲

As you can see, the Gomez ranking is part of a community-oriented site set up to help you comparison-shop. It's a good stop to make before you commit to any one bank for your online services.

Paying Bills Online

Paying bills is right up there with cleaning ovens and putting up storm windows as one of the all-time least popular household tasks. But this distasteful-yet-all-too-necessary activity can be transformed if you do it on the Internet. We won't go so far as to say it will become fun, but it can certainly go from drudgery to downright tolerable work.

There's one good thing about paying bills online: Whether your bank is an Internet all-star, putting every transaction under the sun online, or barely has a functioning Web site, you can pay your bills online. You don't need to use your own bank; there are many banks that will permit those who don't hold accounts there to use their sites to pay bills (you might pay more for the service, however). There are also many non-banks that facilitate bill payment just because they can, such as Yahoo!, which is best known as a search engine. Indeed, bill payment is the cool feature when it comes to banking online. It's offered at many places, it's easy, and everyone who's tried it seems to like it. What's *not* to like about getting out of writing a dozen or so checks every month, hunting down stamps, and trooping off to the post office?

Bits and Bytes: The number of people who pay bills online grew by 68% between 1997 and 1999, according to Dataquest, a research firm in Stamford, Connecticut.

So how does online bill-paying work? In most cases, if you don't have a bank account at the institution or organization you use for bill payment services, you must set up a specialized bill payment account. You will need to be approved for the account because it's a form of credit; the institution will be forwarding your payments to your cable company, electric utility, and wherever else your bills go. This is simply a matter of furnishing the same kind of basic data you'd send to a credit card company.

Then, each month (or however frequently your institution asks) you'll provide funds to cover all your bills. Once you have your account, you give the organization a list of all your creditors, along with your account numbers. This enables the institution to "write the checks" on your behalf. In reality, of course, no checks are written. Instead, payments are disbursed in your name on the date you specify, and sent electronically to the creditor. If a creditor can't or won't accept an electronic funds transfer—such as your landlord, for instance—your bank will cut them an old-fashioned paper check. But you're still off the hook as far as signing and mailing it.

Sound weird? It is, at first. The idea of some huge organization zapping *your* money across the country to your credit card company, your mortgage bank, or whatever other company you owe, without your actual participation is *definitely* weird. But bill payment services let you check each transaction online as it's made, so you can be sure that the right amount was sent on the right date and so on. The main advantage, other than freeing you from writer's cramp and stamp-licking hell, is that each payment is made on the date you specify. This is an excellent feature if you're always racing to the post office on the 15th of each month, mortgage check in hand, desperately trying to avoid yet another late charge. As long as the money's there to cover your payments, your regularly recurring bills (such as mortgages, credit cards, student loans, and so on) will be paid automatically and on time without too much involvement from your end.

Still not convinced? Let's walk through a bill payment setup at Wingspan Bank, a unit of the well-known Bank One Corporation that's being run as an Internet-only bank (although customers can access ATMs owned by Bank One). You don't need an account at Wingspan to use its bill payment service, but it's free if you do. If not, it costs $4.95 a month for the first 10 transactions and 25 cents for each subsequent transaction.

Try It Yourself ▼

1. Go directly to
   http://www.wingspanbank.com/sessionManager/ dispatch?service=BILLPAY.

2. See where it invites you to try out a demo on the third bulleted point? Click on that link.

3. This opens a page called Make Payments. If you were actually paying bills online, this is where you'd enter your payees and the earliest date you'd like them to receive your payments. You'd also enter how much you wanted to pay them and check off a box at the left to indicate they're to be paid. You wouldn't have to do this each month for recurring payments. Go ahead, enter some dummy amounts and check off some boxes. Then click PAY ALL MARKED.

4. Now you get a page called Make Payments—Confirmation, which gives you the payment information to review and asks if you want to go ahead and pay these bills. Click Yes. And that's it. The payments are now scheduled.

Wingspanbank. com is one of a growing number of Internet-only banks.

See how easy it is? Granted, nothing is perfect. In most cases, you can't pay alimony, child support, court-ordered payments, taxes, and other government payments this way. But for the most part, this is an exceptionally easy (and even satisfying) type of online banking transaction.

Plenty of non-banks offer bill payment services as well. By nature, they're all quite similar and relatively inexpensive—banking transactions on the Web cost just pennies to provide compared to ATM, phone, or human-assisted transactions (remember real live tellers?). Yahoo!'s service, for instance, starts at $2 a month plus 40 cents for each payment. Don't fret too much about using a non-bank for these kinds of services. The "front end"—that is, the part of the site you interact with—may not look or act like a bank, but the "back end"—the actual process of settling transactions—is likely to be done the exact same way as a bank, using the same software and other elements. If your trusty bank hasn't shown much inclination to provide online bill payment services, using a non-bank bill payment provider is one way to get on this bandwagon without dealing with a second bank. Who wants more banks than they really need?

Interest Rate Shopping

For more information on getting a mortgage online, see Chapter 10, "Real Estate—Buying and Selling Online."

For more information on student loans online, see Chapter 11, "College—Covering the Skyrocketing Costs of Higher Education."

Apart from conducting bank transactions such as bill paying online, you can use the Internet to shop among services you have every intention of conducting up close and in person. Let's say you want a home equity loan to build that brick patio you've been coveting all these years. Summer is coming, and you can practically taste the lemonade you'll sip under the sun each weekend. You don't want to just march down to your regular old bank and take whatever interest rate they throw at you to finance the construction, but you can't seem to locate any better interest rates by scanning your local newspapers' ads, either.

Don't get impatient and take the first rate you see. There's a variety of Web sites just waiting to feed you the latest on interest rates from banks across the country. (You'd never hear about these banks otherwise because they're hundreds of miles away from you, but they *can* lend you the dough for that patio.) These sites are called *interest rate monitors*. Get to know several of them—you'll find they're useful not just for finding a bank but for obtaining a mortgage or a student loan.

There are several very helpful sites in this area, including Bankrate.com (*http://www.bankrate.com*), Rate.net (*http://www.rate.net*), and BanxQuote (*http://www.banxquote. com*). Each one offers you a sampling of different interest rates for various kinds of bank loans, CDs, and other products.

At Rate.Net, you can search among 11,000 financial institutions, but the information you get isn't limited to list after list. The site throws in its own two cents' worth as well. For instance, it gives daily, quarterly, and annual "Best Rate" awards to the bank that offers the best deal in a given area. Rate.Net also investigates banks' financial stability—although it charges you a membership fee to get this kind of information.

Bankrate.com has a similar objective, but it's a much more comprehensive site that more closely resembles a personal finance portal. It offers news, message boards, expert Q&A columns, commentary, calculators, and all the other categories that can help you manage many aspects of personal finance over the Internet.

On Your Way

Now you have a good sense of how banking has adapted to the Internet. As you know, not all banks are there yet, but a good number of them are pushing their transactions and services online. And even if your bank hasn't exactly embraced the Web yet, you can still do some things, such as bill payment, via other service providers. By now, you should have learned the following:

- Many of the same transactions that can be done in a bank branch or over the telephone can be done easily and with greater privacy online.

- When you're conducting these transactions, you often have greater flexibility and interactivity than you'd have otherwise.

- You should use a rating service to compare the features and attributes of online banks before you make the leap to them.

- Paying bills online is one of the fastest-growing and most popular of all Web transactions, and with good reason—it's easy, inexpensive, can help you manage your finances, and could even become fun.

- It's important to compare interest rates between banks, and several sites exist to help you with this process.

- Be sure that any online bank you use is a member of the Federal Deposit Insurance Corporation (FDIC). For more information on the FDIC and its rules, go to *www.fdic.com*.

CHAPTER 5

Credit and Debt—Taking Care of Your Liabilities Using the Internet

Depending on how you look at credit and debt, they can be either one of the best things about money or one of the worst. If managed well, credit can make it possible for you to make many of your dreams come true—buying a house, going to college, financing a business, and so forth. Credit, which basically means borrowing money, can also help you make it through lean times (hey, we've all had them at one time or another), or simply enable you to buy things sooner than you could otherwise. A credit card can come in mighty handy at the holidays, for example, if you don't have a few hundred dollars sitting around for gifts. That's the good news.

But the flip side of credit is debt, which can be among the biggest—if not *the* biggest—traps in personal finance, not to mention life in general. Debt has this nasty habit of piling up on itself, growing day by day and year by year, along with whatever interest rate you're paying on it, until it can get quite out of control. As you learned in Chapter 3, "Budgeting—Planning for Today and the Future," your financial future can be significantly impeded as long as debt is holding you back.

Not that it's bad to have manageable debt. It's a fact of life. A mortgage counts as debt, and not too many of us can go out and buy a car with cash—customarily, we finance it. Nowadays it's an unusual person who can skate through life without at least some debt. The trick is to handle it responsibly and make sure it stays in proportion to your income and other expenses.

What You'll Learn in This Chapter:

▶ How to find online information about credit cards and unsecured personal loans.

▶ How to obtain your credit history on the Internet.

▶ How to set up a debt reduction plan using Web sites.

So how can the Internet help you with credit and debt? Probably in more ways than you think. As with so many other aspects of personal finance, the Internet's capability to search and sift through literally thousands of bits of information helps you shop among credit providers, whether they're credit card issuers or bank loan providers. And when it comes to debt, all those calculators you've heard so much about can help you assess your debt level and create a plan to pay it down. If you're in too much debt, you can also locate resources via the Internet that can provide non-profit credit counseling and other debt reduction services.

Starting Out: Getting Credit

For most of us, our first experience with credit is a credit card. They're accepted just about everywhere, and junk mail for them clogs our mailboxes day after day. Credit card offers are even routinely mailed out to students barely out of high school. (Shame on you credit card companies!)

Credit cards are a basic form of unsecured credit—that is, you don't need to put up any collateral to the lender in order to receive the card. Essentially, every time you use a credit card you're accepting a loan from the bank, or whichever institution's name is on that card. You're promising to pay that loan back immediately or in monthly increments—of course, generally at a higher interest rate than you'd get if you borrowed money via a secured loan (that is, if you put up some collateral). These high rates protect the lender against the risk that you might hit the road and skip out on your debt, which thousands of credit card customers do every year.

High rates are a reminder that although credit cards are exceptionally easy to obtain for just about everyone, their availability doesn't mean that you don't have to pay it all back. They're real loans. You need to shop around for the best card, just as you would for a loan of any kind. You also have rights and responsibilities with credit cards, just as you'd have if you went to a bank and borrowed a few thousand dollars.

Bankrate.com, a site you just visited in Chapter 4, "Banking Online—Managing Your Money over the Internet," offers a good, basic, unbiased education on credit cards. You'll find it at *http://www.bankrate.com/brm/ccstep.asp*. You can find almost everything you need to know about how credit cards work: the pros and cons of having a credit card, your rights as a cardholder, how to shop for the best card, understanding fixed versus variable interest rates, and so on. The best feature about this guide is that it's unbiased. It's not on some credit card issuer's site, so you know there's no hidden agenda suggesting that credit cards are appropriate for everyone.

If you decide you do want to use credit cards and you plan on carrying a balance, you need to shop around for the best rate. There are several ways to do this. You can be among the fraction of us who actually open each and every one of those unsolicited credit card pitches that show up in the mail. But that's letting selected information come to you rather than your going out and finding the best information. A better way is to use the Internet for comparison shopping of rates. You can find this information online at the comprehensive interest rate sites discussed at the end of Chapter 4, but there are other sites that specialize in credit card rates and comparison shopping. These Web sites are more useful because of their narrow focus on this particular area of finance.

Let's try one. Open your browser to *http://www.cardweb.com*. This is CardWeb, which has some rather lofty ambitions (it calls itself the "global payment card information network"). It's *quite* helpful. Here, you can read detailed news on the credit card industry if you're particularly interested in the ins and outs of the business, but more importantly, you can access a ton of information on credit cards from various card providers, name by name and bank by bank. Now you're no longer reliant on whichever credit card junk mail shows up in your mailbox; rather, you can take control of the search for the credit card that's best for you.

*Sites like
CardWeb.com
help you find the
best credit card
deal for your
needs.*

This site does monthly surveys of specific low-rate and
no-annual-fee cards, broken down into standard, gold, and plat-
inum. It also surveys the myriad varieties of cards: secured cards
(ideal for anyone with impaired credit or no history of credit;
unlike most credit cards, you have to post collateral in order to
obtain them), affinity cards, reward cards, credit union cards, and
business credit cards. One particularly nice feature of CardWeb is
CardLocator, a database of credit card issuers that you can search
by entering your state. This way you'll get not only national card
issuers, but local ones too. Finally, there's a message board where
consumers can exchange gripes and tips about various credit card
providers, apart from what the experts say.

What if you don't want to use credit cards—perhaps the tempta-
tion to whip them out for unnecessary purchases is too strong—
but you need to finance some things in your life anyway? You can
get an unsecured personal loan directly from a bank. These loans
are few and far between nowadays because credit cards have risen
in popularity over the last couple of decades, but they're still out
there. In fact, because these loans are so rare nowadays, the

Internet is a particularly good way to locate them. For a basic primer on unsecured bank loans, go to another page on Bankrate's Web site: *http://www.bankrate.com/brm/green/perloan/ perloan1a.asp*. Once you're up to speed on how unsecured loans work, you can use the same site to locate banks that offer unsecured personal loans at various interest rates. A word of warning on these loans: It's often better to get a credit card because the rates can be lower, and you can simply tuck it away when you're not using it. Unsecured personal loans aren't necessarily your cheapest form of credit.

Credit Histories 101

You can't go out and borrow money for the big stuff—a house or a car, for example—without first demonstrating to lenders that you've managed to handle credit in the past without getting into trouble. This is called building a *credit history*, a record of your prior dealings with credit that shows how quickly (or slowly) you paid off debt, how much credit you've been extended, and so forth. Your credit history also includes an assessment of your prior ability to pay bills, such as electric bills and rent, and if you've ever had your overdue account turned over to a collection agency. All this goes into your credit history.

Credit histories are maintained in the form of credit reports by credit rating agencies, which list how much you owe and how fast or slowly you've paid back borrowed money to any company you've done business with. When you apply for a loan, the potential lender contacts these credit agencies to get the lowdown on how you've handled credit. Usually, information stays in your report for seven years, after which it generally disappears from your report.

The Internet is a good way to interact with credit bureaus, which are about as pleasant to deal with as your local DMV. Before the Internet came along, most people never saw their credit reports until they really needed them, such as when they were about to buy a house. At that point, it's a little late to fix anything that might be wrong on your report (and indeed, credit rating agencies make plenty of mistakes). But with the Internet, you can see your credit report anytime you want—before you buy a house or car, or perhaps just when the mood hits you (hey, you never know... you might want to find out what people are saying about you). No matter how much debt you have, most of it is on record with the credit rating agencies. But the good news is that you have a legal right to know what's on your record. In fact, you have many rights when it comes to credit. Fortunately, tons of information on these rights is available online as well.

Let's start by visiting a site that serves as a consumer advocate on credit, acting on your behalf if you feel your credit report is wrong or you're being unfairly treated by a credit reporting agency. It's the Credit Information Center, at *http://www.creditinfocenter.com*. Here, you'll find everything from basic legal information to stories about people who sued credit rating agencies (and even won). You can also surf the Consumer Credit Counseling Services (CCCS) bulletin boards, take an interactive debt test, find out about debt consolidation services, and get general information on being in debt—hey, we've all been there!

The site can give you some pretty specific advice, ranging from how to check the statute of limitations on debt to negotiating your credit rating and coping with collection agencies. This site also provides ammunition for fighting a credit reporting agency. There's information on the Fair Credit Reporting Act, which not only says you have the right to see your report but also governs the behavior of credit reporting and collection agencies. The FCRA permits you to dispute inaccurate information in your credit history and have it changed or deleted. *Accurate* information cannot be changed or deleted, contrary to what some credit clinics like to advertise.

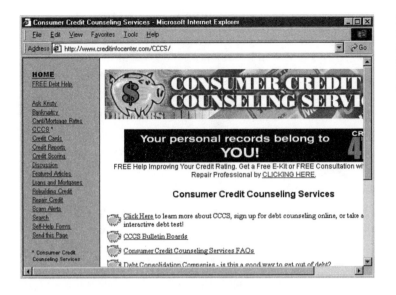

The Consumer Credit Counseling Services offer lots of help to aid you in managing your credit and debt.

Now that you know where to find information about your rights when it comes to credit, you're probably dying to see what's in that report. No problem. A tidy little industry has developed around making your credit reports available online—for a price, usually. The prices aren't steep, however—a fairly typical tab is less than $10—and the speed with which you receive your little dossier makes it well worth the price. At *http://www.banksite.com*, for instance, your report will cost $8, but you will get a detailed multipage report on your screen within 30 seconds (or so the site promises). That's fantastic if you're too antsy to wait a few days and have it mailed to you, or if you're in the midst of applying for a loan online on some other site. You'll be asked to enter quite specific and detailed personal information, such as your previous addresses, credit card account numbers, Social Security number, and employer's name. And you're required to agree to the site's privacy policy.

Another Web site like this is *http://www.credit411.com*, which aims to provide a "secure and simple process for obtaining credit reports." It's a little more commercial than Banksite.com, and it encourages you to get three separate reports from three separate credit reporting agencies—a hard sales pitch if we've ever seen one. Although it's possible that your reports could be significantly different from agency to agency, unless you suspect that errors have been made, it's usually sufficient just to get your report from one agency.

Finally, steer clear of offers for free copies of your credit report. These will pop up from time to time, but they're almost always lame attempts to sell you something, such as a loan.

So You're In Debt: Join the Club

At some point in just about anyone's life, they have some debt. If you do too, relax a bit. Some red ink is normal. The key is managing it so that eventually you're in the black, or at least you have a handle on the debt you've agreed to live with. What *isn't* great is a chunk of debt that never goes away, and what *isn't* normal is so much debt that you're struggling to make ends meet. Whether you fall into one category or another, it's a good idea to have some kind of debt reduction plan.

You've already learned about the calculators available on the Internet that can help you assess how much debt you have and show you how that debt is holding you back. Now let's look at planners and calculators that can help you plan a strategy for getting out of debt. Rev up your browser and head to iVillage, which features a nifty debt reduction planner in its MoneyLife section. In order to use the planner, though, you have to become a member. It's free, so do that first. Go to *http://www.ivillagemoneylife. com/money/articles/0,4029,12462~365,00.html*.

iVillage offers an excellent debt reduction planner that will help you understand what you owe and how to get out of debt.

Let's plug in some numbers and see what happens.

1. Click Launch the Planner at the center of the page. It may take a moment for the planner to load, depending on your computer.

2. Following the directions at the top, choose one of the links to find out more about why you might need to reconsider your debts. (You'll get an explanation in the gray box on the right.) Then click Next.

3. Enter your debt information as requested. As you enter each debtor, the list to the right will grow. When you're finished, click Next.

4. Now that you've got an estimate of when you're going to be out of debt, based on your balance, interest rate, and how much you're paying off each month, you're invited to create an action plan to pay off your debt more quickly. Click Next to do so.

5. Here, you're taught how to optimize your payments by paying off the debts with the highest interest rates first and keeping your total debt payments the same. Once you pay off one debtor, don't slack off! Apply that money to the next debt, and so on.

▼ **Try It Yourself**

6. Next, enter how much of your savings you want to apply toward debt. You're told that it's often helpful to use savings to pay down debt, because the interest rates on debt are almost always higher than they'd be in a savings account. Enter this information now, and click Next when finished.

7. Now, see how much you can reduce your expenses by entering a dollar amount. Click Next again.

8. Finally, you get a chart with two lines: your old plan in blue and your new debt reduction plan in green. The dates at the bottom show when you can expect to be debt-free using this plan!

▲

Overheard:

In 1997, a record 1.8 million Americans called the National Foundation for Consumer Credit's member agencies for help. The number one reason they needed help with debt was overspending, followed by job loss, medical problems, and divorce or separation.

The last screen gives you some rules in the form of steps. For instance, it may sound obvious, but don't rack up more debt as you're trying to pay down your current debt. You can also get a payment schedule for the first year of your new plan.

As another option with a similar objective, you should also try out Quicken.com's Debt Reduction Planner. This is a feature developed by Quicken that is often licensed to other companies, such as banks and finance companies. It is linked from their site to others (such as Wells Fargo Bank at *http://www.wellsfargo.com/ per/planner/debt/info/*). This planner, which works very much like iVillage's tool, asks you for information on your current debt, offers a plan to get you out of debt, and gives you an action plan.

Sometimes, the debt really enters dangerous territory. You might be painfully aware that you've got too much debt, or you might have it sneak up on you—maybe you don't even realize it until you use one of these Internet calculators or planners. Regardless, if you're in too much debt, you might need some additional help to get out of it.

There are countless debt counseling services out there, many of which are profit-minded companies that will charge a fee for information you can get for nothing elsewhere. Naturally, these companies have colonized the Internet and set up sites all over the place, so be careful of their pitches. You'll know them when you see them, popping up as banner ads (those long horizontal ads that show up on almost every Web site these days) or as irresistible pitches sent to your email box. Instead, turn to a general, nonprofit source of online debt crisis management, such as the sites run by the National Foundation for Consumer Credit (at *http://www.nfcc.org*) and Debt Counselors (at *http://www.dca.org*). The NFCC is a network of 1,450 nonprofit agencies that provide money management education and budget and debt counseling. They can even help you set up a repayment plan for all your creditors. The site isn't as comprehensive as you might like, but it's a good introduction to the NFCC's services and includes a directory of NFCC members you can call.

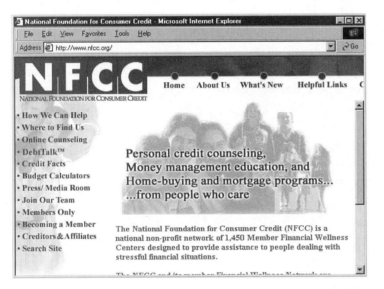

The NFCC is a nonprofit organization that helps people get out of debt.

More Help with Debt

If you realize you need help to get out of debt, consider a debt consolidation plan. This is actually a new loan intended to bundle all your debt into one monthly payment, ideally at a lower interest rate than some of the loans you're now paying. Naturally, you'll pay a fee to consolidate your debts this way.

GetSmart.com, at *http://www.getsmart.com*, can match you up with debt consolidation services and provide links to lenders.

Founded by a group of former bankers, the site is basically a search engine for debt consolidators (and regular loans as well). You can enter basic data connected to your current debt situation and get an email response from potential debt consolidators.

Debt consolidation "services" (again, basically loans) certainly aren't for everyone. It helps if you own a home, for instance, in which case your loan would probably be a home equity loan. And you can get home equity loans just as easily without going to a debt consolidation service.

If you don't own a home, you're best off eliminating your debts on your own by paying off the costliest debts first, which is a form of consolidation. Here's how to do it: First, identify the maximum amount you can put toward your debts each month. Then, find the debt with the highest interest rate and put more of your funds toward that one each month, no matter how big that high-rate debt is, and even if it means paying just the minimum amount owed on the others. As soon as the highest-rate debt is completely eliminated, go on to the next highest and do the same thing with it. Keep working down from one debt to the next this way. But whatever you do, don't cut down on the total amount you pay on your debts; just keep applying it to the highest rates first. Eventually, you'll just face the lower-rate debts, which add up more slowly and are more manageable than those with higher interest rates. Reward yourself along the way, perhaps quarterly, by treating yourself to something fun—without going into debt to do it, of course.

On Your Way

You've seen that credit and debt are two unavoidable pieces of your overall personal finance picture. Credit can be useful, but if it's used unwisely it turns into too much debt, which can be a disaster. By now you should have learned the following:

- Using credit cards isn't for everyone, but if you decide you want to use them, you can get some basic information and do some comparison shopping on the Internet.

- You have a basic right to know what's contained in your credit history, and there are a number of sites on the Internet that will make your credit report available to you for a small fee. Similarly, there are sites that will inform you of your rights under the Fair Credit Reporting Act.

- It makes sense to approach debt with a plan for getting your payments into shape, and several sites contain debt reduction planners for this purpose.

PART III

Building and Protecting Your Wealth

CHAPTER 6

Insurance—Finding the Best Policy Online

Every person and family needs to be properly insured. Whether it's for a car, a house, your life, or merely the contents of a two-room apartment, insurance is necessary to ensure that some nasty unforeseen event doesn't wipe out you and your family financially.

Buying insurance can be a confusing mess. It seems as if there are as many kinds of insurance as there are things to protect. Some insurance is required by a creditor or by law—fire and homeowners' insurance, for instance, and certain kinds of auto insurance. Other kinds are just plain smart to have, such as flood insurance if you live in a flood zone, or life insurance for you and your spouse. And for every type of insurance out there, hundreds of insurance providers compete to sell you a policy or two. If you let it, choosing insurance can be among the most bewildering and frustrating aspects of your personal finance. Yet if you let it slide, you'll probably regret it.

Along came the Internet and be glad it did. Coping with insurance online is a lot easier, and sometimes better, than dealing with it exclusively through agents or the insurance companies themselves. For one thing, you have access to more information about these products than ever before—forget about the days when shopping for insurance meant calling up agent after agent and listening to their spiels before you could even get a quote. As for that persistent insurance agent who wants to elbow his way into your home some evening and pull up a chair at your kitchen table for a two-hour sales pitch? Tell him to hit the road. Not only can you shop for insurance online, but you can find out all you need

What You'll Learn in This Chapter:

▶ How to learn about basic types of insurance policies using informational Web sites.

▶ How to compare quotes from different insurance providers online.

▶ How to gauge your insurance company's financial well-being and stability.

▶ How to apply for a policy online.

to know about a basic policy and apply for it via the Internet as well. It's still handy to have an insurance agent around if you have specific questions, but the days of relying on those guys from soup to nuts are gone.

A Crash Course in Insurance

Before you buy an insurance policy, it makes sense to educate yourself on the kinds you may need because each kind has its own jargon. Obviously, fire insurance and auto insurance are a lot different (as well they should be). Just because you've bought one kind of insurance in the past doesn't necessarily mean you have a clue about another kind.

You can educate yourself on different kinds of policies by going to educational sites run by insurance organizations, visiting personal finance portals with insurance sections, and even reading up on insurance at the insurance companies' sites. At this point you're just looking for background information, so don't worry too much if you wind up studying the merits of, say, flood insurance by reading through State Farm's site. You're going to get credible information from a variety of sites.

However, it might make sense to start out with a general, unbiased site run by a trade group of insurance companies, such as the Insurance Information Institute. This organization, a trade group of insurance companies, makes it its business to inform the rest of us on the ins and outs of insurance. It's very useful information. The Institute's Web site—go ahead, pull it up at *http://www.iii.org*—takes you through the different parts of a given type of insurance policy, defining the terms specific to that kind of insurance.

When it comes down to actually shopping for a policy and comparing specific insurers' products, knowing this jargon can be invaluable. For example, the Institute's What's In an Auto Policy? page guides you through each element, such as bodily injury liability, personal injury protection, property damage liability, collision, and so on. For each kind of insurance, the site also includes relevant background information. For auto insurance, it offers a piece on deer/car collisions (complete with tips for avoiding such an unfortunate experience), as well as state-by-state guidelines for teen drivers' permits. This is the kind of useful stuff that could take hours to track down separately.

The Insurance Information Institute's Web site is an excellent place to find information about products and insurance lingo.

This is helpful information, but what if you just want to home in on a particular type of insurance? In that case, you might want to visit sites run by more specialized trade groups for certain kinds of insurance. For instance, the American Council of Life Insurance has its own site at *http://www.acli.com*. Likewise, the Health Insurance Association of America has a site at *http://www.hiaa.org*. No doubt you'll find others.

Just keep a few things in mind before you start surfing. First of all, these organizations represent specific kinds of insurance companies—and these companies wouldn't bother paying their dues to these groups if they didn't expect some serious promotional efforts in return. In other words, don't bounce over to the ACLI site expecting a serious discussion of the merits of life insurance. You won't get it. What you will get is a big dose of "why life insurance is so wonderful." Also, in some cases these sites are dreadfully dull and geared a bit more toward hardcore insurance types—insurance agents who make it their business to know every detail and really care about it. Unless you really want to delve into these topics full-bore (pun intended!), you might be better off using the data that's available on more general sites, such as the Insurance Information Institute's.

Policy, Here We Come

Okay, now that you're all set on the basics of various kinds of insurance, you're ready to find a policy. You need to compare prices—you'll hear them referred to as *quotes*—as well as specific features in a policy. However, many policies have very similar features and differ mostly in price.

Not to worry. The Internet has a wealth of sites that can find insurance quotes for you, as well as match you up with agents who'd be only too happy to back up those quotes with actual sales. If you're not averse to hooking up with an insurance agent, let's jump right in and go to one of those sites: *http://www.insuranceagents.com*.

First, go to the selection bars on the bottom. Select the type of insurance you want to buy and the state where you live. You get a blurb describing that kind of insurance, and then you're asked to provide some basic information that affects the pricing—such as, for life insurance, whether or not you smoke. The site lists independent agents who are part of the network who can sell insurance in your state. The site promises that an agent will contact you with a quote. Easy, huh?

Would you prefer to contact the agents yourself? You can go straight to the agents themselves by going to the Independent Insurance Agents of America site at *http://www.independentagent.com/*. (Hey, in this business it seems like everyone has a group!) After going to the Agent Locator selection (available straight from the home page), just enter in your state and your ZIP code to get lists of agents. Then it's up to you to contact an agent if you want.

But chances are you're going to prefer shopping among the policies themselves, free of any agent pushing one policy over another. Remember, this freedom to compare without sales pressure is one of the Internet's best attributes when it comes to shopping for insurance. For this, you might try one of a few different insurance policy search engines. It's no surprise that these sites are proliferating, given the thousands of insurance policies available out there and the competition in the industry to sell them (not to mention that just about all of us need to buy insurance at some point).

One of the best of these insurance shopping sites is *http://www.insweb.com*. Let's see how easy it is to shop on this site.

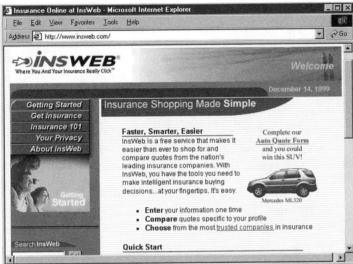

InsWeb is one of the best and easiest ways to compare coverage and costs without the sales pressure of an agent.

▼ Try It Yourself

1. Go to the InsWeb home page. In the middle of the page, you see Quick Start, with a choice of a few different kinds of insurance. There you can indicate whether you're a new or returning user. Select New to InsWeb and fill out the form (you just need to enter your email address and create a password). Submit the form.

2. Now you have a page with those choices of different insurance products again. For your foray into this site today, try auto insurance. Click on the car.

3. Now you're invited to shop for quotes. You're told it will take 15 to 20 minutes to enter your information: current policy, vehicle registration, and so on. Yes, that's a serious time commitment. But "our customers tell us it's worth it!", says

InsWeb. Give the site the benefit of the doubt and go for it. At the end of this process, you can review quotes. The number of quotes you get is determined by your personal information, as well as the state you live in—not all insurers write policies for all states.

4. Fill out the form, which asks for conventional auto insurance information (your occupation, driving history, and so on). Keep going.

5. Now fill in the data about your vehicle. Choose the make and model of your car. Continue.

6. Now you're asked for purchase and registration information on the car, as well as information on how it's used, your driving habits, and any other specific considerations. For instance, do you have an alarm on the car? At any point in filling out the form, you can call a toll-free phone number if you need help.

7. Specify what type of coverage you want: liability levels for bodily injury, collision, medical payment coverage, and so on, as well as the deductibles you'd like to pay on the vehicle. Fill in this information and keep going.

8. Now you're back to some personal information about your residence and prior insurance coverage of this kind.

9. Here, the site asks you to search for any "affinity groups" that could help you get a deal on your insurance. An affinity group could be something like membership in the American Automobile Association or the American Association of Retired Persons.

10. Now you're in business. The page lists companies that are prepared to give you insurance quotes, complete with their logos and their ratings from A.M. Best and Standard & Poor's (we'll go into more detail on why that's important in a moment). The last few steps just require you to verify a few things, such as your name and address.

If you need a deep breath after all of this, you're not alone. But this kind of comprehensiveness is what makes InsWeb so helpful. Unlike some sites that barely ask you for any information and then purport to give you a "quote" based on the sketchiest of details, you can rest assured that InsWeb's quotes are close to the real thing.

The biggest drawback to InsWeb isn't so much the time involved to use it as that, to some degree, the site does not serve everyone. For example, if you live in New Jersey and want to shop for auto insurance, you're out of luck. The site won't quote you rates for auto insurance in that state, explaining that new companies and states are being added steadily. You find out when you select the state from the scroll bar.

Finally, when you're shopping for different insurance policies, at some point you'll probably find it pretty useful to see how these products are described by the insurers themselves. For that, you can check out their Web sites. As you'd expect, the sites are the Web's equivalent of glossy, thick-stock advertisements: uniformly slick and polished, easy on the eyes, and heavy on the pitch. But they may also give you detailed information on the policies you're considering, as well as answers to your questions about the insurance company, contact information for agents, and price information (if you haven't already gotten some quotes). And if you need to make a claim someday, in most cases you can figure out how to do so by going to these sites.

Doing Due Diligence

Before you buy any insurance policy, however, you should check out the financial stability of the insurance company—that is, perform a little "due diligence" on it. This means knowing all about the insurer's financial strength and future ability to pay out a claim to you (in the unfortunate event that you need one).

Why do due diligence? After all, you don't normally investigate a company's finances before you buy a product from it. Well, most companies aren't run like insurance companies. They run their business by taking in premiums—the money you pay to keep the insurance coverage for any given period—and investing that money, often in the stock market. The costs of those premiums are decided by that complicated and mind-numbing process known as *underwriting*, or figuring out how likely it is that a given group of people will actually need to make claims at some point in the future. The insurance company assumes that a certain number of claims will always be filed, and those claims are paid for out of the premiums that are invested. Ideally for everyone, there will be far fewer claims than premiums, and the insurance company can pocket some profits while the people who do file claims get paid.

Unfortunately, however, not all insurance companies are equally good at figuring out how to underwrite, not to mention how to invest all those premiums. In some cases, an insurance company can run into big problems if it gets hit with claims that it can't pay—either because the claims outpace the premiums or the underlying investments weren't chosen very well and lost money. Bottom line: An insurance company's financial stability and ability to pay claims has a great deal to do with its quality, and that's something that you should investigate before purchasing a policy.

Fortunately, to make this process easier, there's a whole industry based on rating insurance companies. These insurance raters attach grades based on how stable companies are. For instance, an A++ rating indicates a tip-top company from which you should have no qualms about buying a policy. On the other hand, a company rated C- should give you pause. To your benefit, the biggest insurance raters—A.M. Best, Standard & Poor's, and Weiss Ratings (our favorite)—have placed this information on the Internet free of charge, making your due diligence a far easier process than it used to be.

Let's look at A.M. Best's site. Go to the home page at *http://www.ambest.com/*. Here, you can search for each insurer's latest rating.

You can find out how stable and solvent your insurance carrier is at sites such as A.M. Best.

1. On the home page, you'll see a variety of options, each with several links below it. Under the Rating Information option, choose the link marked Ratings Search.

2. Now you see a simple informational form asking you to give A.M. Best some data about yourself and your search. Don't worry—A.M. Best isn't trying to sell you anything. It's just asking for information about the types of people searching its site. (Can't blame them for that, can you?) Fill in this information and submit the form.

3. On the next page, you have another blank form asking for your search criteria, specifically the name of the insurance company you're inquiring about. For the purposes of this exercise, enter State Farm.

4. Now you've got a list of various State Farm units. Don't worry about the fact that there is more than one; an insurance company this big can have units, or "domiciles," based in more than one county and state. Each domicile might be for a different branch of the insurance company. In this case, it's State Farm's life insurance and indemnity units. The A.M. Best ratings appear in the yellow box over on the right.

▼ **Try It Yourself**

Simply look for the rating that corresponds to the unit with which you'll be doing business. If you're not sure, assess all the ratings. They should all be somewhat similar... maybe a scattering of A++'s mixed in with some A's. You get the idea—the higher the ranking, the better the company.

Another, very different way to suss out any possible hints of trouble at a given insurance company—or simply find answers to questions about a specific insurer or type of policy—is to find any dirt on it at the Insurance News Network site (*http://www.insure.com*), which bills itself as the "consumer insurance guide."

When you want the inside scoop on an insurer, a good place to look is insure.com.

This is quite a comprehensive Web site, so you should spend some time here. It's certainly worth visiting, both before and after settling on a policy and after the purchase, just to catch up on any issues related to insurance. It has lots of news related to insurance, as well as information on special investigations and probes into insurance practices. A good service called Complaint Finder, found just off the home page, enables you to investigate complaint rankings compiled by state insurance departments. Each state has an insurance department to make sure that insurers write policies that comply with regulations. Occasionally some companies—usually lower-rated ones—will run afoul of such regulations.

The site also has useful forums on subjects such as auto theft, home insurance, and so on. Users can post very specific questions, which are then saved and archived along with their answers. For example, one visitor asked, "I had to take off work to pick up my stolen car. Will my insurer pay for my lost wages?" (Answer: Not in most cases.) You can scroll down through dozens of past questions and answers, some of them quite long and detailed. Who else could answer these questions? It's kind of like having a state insurance commissioner sitting in your living room... or home office, or wherever you do this stuff.

Senior Specials

If you or someone dear to you is coming up on age 65, that milestone brings a whole host of insurance questions. Seniors will find themselves being pitched specialized insurance products, such as Medigap insurance and long-term care insurance (basically, insurance to pay for stays in assisted-living and nursing home facilities, or for at-home living assistance should they require it). And hitting age 65 also brings up a number of questions about Medicare, the government's health insurance program for the elderly. In some cases, you'll be contacted about some of these products, particularly long-term care insurance, well before age 65. It makes sense to bone up on insurance products, specifically as they relate to senior-citizenship.

One site that will help make this learning process a little easier is Senior Resource, found at *http://www.seniorresource.com/insur.htm*. It has great outlines and definitions of the different types of insurance that seniors are likely to encounter, presented in no-nonsense black-and-white—literally. This site also has useful links to other insurance resources, such as companies that specialize in life insurance for seniors.

A Policy in Hand

Now that you've found information on the types of insurance you may need, seen a few quotes, located the actual policy you think works for you, and done your due diligence on the company providing it, about all that's left is to buy the policy itself.

Remember how we said you can do away with pesky insurance agents knocking on your door? That's because, in addition to the resources that individual agents have put online (many of them have chosen to create Web sites of their own to promote their businesses and pitch their services), quite a few big insurance companies now permit you to apply directly via the Internet. Some of them will even grant you substantial premium discounts for applying or buying online. Granted, to complete an application for some kinds of insurance, you may still need to have someone visit you in person—but it won't be for a sales call as much as to close a deal you've already started. Considering how entrenched the insurance agent's role has been in the insurance industry, this is quite a revolution.

Let's sample how easy it is to apply for a policy online, using John Hancock's site as a try-out. For illustration's sake, pretend that you're interested in a term life insurance policy. Open your browser and go to *http://www.johnhancock.com*.

Try It Yourself ▼

1. Over on the left you see a menu bar. The fifth item down from the top is labeled Buy Direct. That's you—go for it.

2. You're now in what John Hancock calls MarketPlace. Scroll down a bit. Below the Here's What We Offer at MarketPlace header, you'll see several choices. Select the one marked Start the application process.

3. You're now told to begin by getting a quote, and you're asked to fill in a straightforward form below. The site includes a disclaimer saying that the quote is for "reference only" and that it could change due to the more rigorous underwriting that the insurance company will do later. Remember, you're just *applying* online; nothing is guaranteed yet. For this reason, the information needed to get the quote is very simple. Fill it in and click Get Quote.

4. Almost immediately, you're presented with a bright yellow box containing your quote. At the bottom of the page are three options: Start Online, Call Me Now (if you decide to bail out of the online application process, John Hancock doesn't want to lose you; it wants you to dial up one of its reps instead), and Start By Phone (same idea). Click Start Online.

5. You get a screen outlining the nine-step application process, with a particularly handy feature—a guide to how many minutes you can expect each portion to take. Remember how long it took to enter that quote information on the InsWeb site? It's pretty smart for John Hancock to give us fair warning of what we're getting into, timewise. The site also tells you that you'll need to have your driver's license, doctor's address, and other insurance-related information as part of the process.

There's no need to walk you through each part of the process—it's fairly lengthy, and you get the idea by now. If you were to finish the application and submit it to Hancock, later you'd be contacted by a rep to set up an interview and complete the insurance sale. As you can see, the Internet doesn't necessarily replace every single step of the insurance-buying process, but it can greatly simplify what used to be a complicated and bewildering transaction for most of us.

On Your Way

You've seen that buying insurance can be a daunting process, fraught with huge volumes of information in a competitive marketplace. Now you know that a revolution has taken place on the Internet. The old ways of buying and selling insurance are yielding to a newer, more accessible way to review policies, check out insurance companies, and even apply online:

- It's easy to get a basic education on insurance by using general insurance sites.

- You can compare insurance policies and get quotes without ever setting foot in an insurance agency.

- It's important to know about your insurance company's financial soundness.

- More and more big insurance companies are letting customers apply for and even buy insurance directly via the Internet.

CHAPTER 7

Taxes—Internet Resources to Help You Keep More of Your Money

Nobody likes taxes—nobody. For anyone who's ever earned a paycheck, made a successful investment, inherited a few bucks, or basically had anything at all to do with bringing in some cash, taxes go along for the ride. Yeah, sure, taxes bring us all the municipal, state, and federal services we need and enjoy— schools, police, fire departments, parks, and so on. But must taxes—and more to the point, *paying* taxes—be such a huge pain in the neck?

Well, we can't guarantee that you'll ever like taxes—that's asking a little too much—but the Internet can go a long, long way toward making all things tax-related a little more bearable. The Internet's most helpful qualities, such as its capability to provide buckets and buckets of data with relative ease and speed, go hand-in-hand with something as complicated as taxes. Gone are the days of trooping off to your post office or bank branch for tax forms— with a few mouse clicks, you can download just about any tax form directly to your computer and print it out yourself. Say goodbye to sifting through dusty old tax guides at your local library for hours on end—you can easily browse the Internal Revenue Service's publications on your desktop. As for tax counseling, the Internet plays host to literally thousands of enterprising accountants who are eager for your business. So, the good news is that the proper use of the Internet has made taxpaying a whole lot less stressful.

What You'll Learn in This Chapter:

▶ How to find sites that tell you how taxes work.

▶ How to download the tax forms you need.

▶ How to calculate the impact of taxes on your assets.

▶ What's involved in electronic tax filing.

▶ How to start forming an overall tax strategy.

▶ How to find an accountant online.

Bits and Bytes:

Don't take any tax advice you receive online without checking it out first with your tax professional.

That said, we have a few words of warning when it comes to taxes and the Internet. For some reason that we can't exactly figure out, the Internet has encouraged the creation of many quirky Web sites on the subject of taxes. Some are merely strange. Others are political, such as the sites run by Citizens United to Reform the Economy and Citizens for Tax Justice, two groups that aim to completely reform how we pay our taxes. Nothing wrong with that, but you won't find much meaningful tax information there. Still other sites are downright misleading or dangerous, offering advice that may be completely wrong. It seems that, because taxes inspire such angst for most of us, many enterprising people are selling tax-related services online, often disguising their pitches as genuine tax education or consumer assistance. When it comes to taxes, the Internet can get pretty sleazy pretty fast.

For more information on personal finance portals, see Chapter 2, "How Can I Use the Internet for Personal Finance?"

Beware! One site we found offers a nice little range of services, such as a tax review, a hotline, "strategic tax" audiotapes, and a quarterly newsletter—for the tidy sum of $598 a year. You could get essentially the same information, minus the tapes, for free by using Web sites that are oriented toward the consumer, not sales. These sites include personal finance portals, many of which excel at tax information and often beef up their tax sections with timely articles and coverage of new tax issues. Other sites are set up just around tax information. Either way, you shouldn't have to pay anyone for good online tax information, so be wary of the many tax hucksters on the Internet.

Along the same lines, as you navigate the Internet's tax resources, you will no doubt encounter many tantalizing offers to help you file your taxes electronically, locate missing tax refunds, and other similar appeals. Naturally, you should be as careful with these as you would with any salesperson. Many of them are vendors that simply want to sell you a service. (By the way, you can file your taxes electronically on your own quite easily, thank you, with a little assistance from the IRS's site, which you'll be reading about shortly.) Others are run by well-meaning accountants who happen to take an aggressive approach. Their sites might actually contain some fairly useful tax-related information, but you might find a hefty dose of salesmanship as well.

Getting Started

So, you can take a big bold step out of the dark ages into a brave new world, one of enlightenment and—maybe for the first time— a real understanding of how your taxes work. Great. Let's get started by visiting a few sites that offer good general information about taxes.

There are quite a few general informational sites on the subject. As we said, those trusty portals do a lot in this area. SmartMoney's site features dozens of articles archived under the Tax Matters heading. You'll also find new articles on the site's home page, usually one or two a week, simply by scrolling down the middle of the page. Even more useful is the site's Tax Guide at *http://www.smartmoney.com/ac/tax/*. It has primers on separate topics, such as capital gains taxes and retirement taxes.

Other good general information sites aren't necessarily portals, such as the one run by Fairmark Press at *http://www.fairmark.com/*. It claims to be "the Internet's plain lan- guage tax guide." Granted, Fairmark has good reason to go to such lengths; it's a publisher of tax guides for consumers and would like to sell you a few books. But get past that pitch—and fortunately, it's not too heavy-handed—and you'll find a wealth of information. The site reviews books about taxes (as well as other aspects of personal finance), lists tax rate schedules, and offers a useful message board for chatting about taxes (no, that may not sound too scintillating, but check it out on April 15 or so).

Fairmark's site also takes an interesting approach to taxes and tax information. As we all know, taxes affect just about every aspect of personal finance, from saving money to spending it to investing it. But do you know how taxes affect a particular financial tool, such as a Roth IRA? Wouldn't having that information help you decide whether or not to open a Roth IRA? The Fairmark site can walk you through the pros and cons of the Roth IRA from a tax perspective. Clearly marked along the way are links to even more tax information about the Roth. This is just an example of the gold mine of tax information at this site, not to mention general retirement savings information.

For more informa- tion on IRAs, see Chapter 12, "Retirement— Planning and Financing Your Golden Years."

*A commercial site
run by Fairmark
Press offers news,
chat rooms, and
reviews of tax
guides.*

Still hungry for tax information? You might be surprised to know
that the IRS has a very useful Web site for its legions of fans at
http://www.irs.gov/. Yes, the IRS, that old bureaucracy we all love
so much. The site is well worth visiting for several reasons. For
one, you can download just about every single federal tax form
you'll ever need—we'll talk about how to do that in a moment.
You can also read any of the dozens of free IRS guidebooks,
which explain the IRS tax code on everything from business
deductions to filing when you're self-employed. They're particularly useful if you don't use an accountant but instead wade
through your own taxes every year.

**And they called it
progress...**

Pennsylvania's state
constitution of 1776
established taxpay-
ing as the qualifica-
tion for voting,
supplanting the tra-
ditional test of prop-
erty ownership.

The IRS site is also the online authority on tax exemptions and
deductions—everyone's favorite thing about taxes (well, we have
to like *something* about taxes, don't we?)—as well as on tax ter-
minology and electronic filing. The site even has a sense of
humor. Not only is the home page decidedly funny, with an old-
fashioned newspaper gimmick (called The Digital Daily), but
there's also Braintaxer, an interactive game show that quizzes you
on various IRS programs. Hey, some rainy afternoon, you might
give it a shot. (Get a life!)

Downloading Tax Forms

So you're ready to get down to business and think about paying your taxes. Let's see how easy it is to download your tax forms from the Internet. This is one of the most useful things you can do online when it comes to taxes.

Start by figuring out your federal forms. You'll see offers all over the Internet for free federal form downloads, but perhaps the best source for downloading these babies is the IRS. Why is the IRS better than other sites? The forms are the same, but you might find that some sites don't update their forms on a timely basis. When you're all set to hunker down with this year's forms, the last thing you want to do is download a form from last year by mistake. Moreover, some sites just offer common forms, whereas the IRS has made all of its forms available in one location so you don't have to wander around trying to locate what you need.

Let's walk through it now so you'll see exactly what we mean. Fire up your browser and go to the IRS home page, *http://www.irs.gov/*.

1. As you can see, the IRS home page is a colorful rendition of a fictional newspaper… what fun! But we're all business. Skip the hijinks and scroll down to the bottom of the page to a selection of links. See the one labeled Forms and Pubs? Click on that to go to the next page.

   ▼ **Try It Yourself**

2. Now you're at a page with quite a selection of forms and publications. On the left you see the heading Download Current Year Forms and Publications. This is what you want. Below that heading is an array of options. Now you know why you came here for forms—you can select them according to various parameters, such as by date or number, or you can see all of them at once on one big scroll bar. And by the way, you can even download previous years' tax forms if you're doing some catch-up work. For now, take a look at everything that's available and select from there. Just click on the first option, called Forms and Instructions.

3. You now have a brief set of instructions for downloading your forms. You need to pick the format in which your forms will be sent to your computer. Fill in the blank next to the format you want. Below that is a big list of all the IRS forms. As you can see, there's every form you can imagine, ranging from such beauties as Form W-2AS American Samoa Wage and Tax Statement to the ever-popular Form 6478 Credit for Alcohol Used as Fuel. But let's skip the exotic stuff and scroll down to an old standby: Form 1040 U.S. Individual Income Tax Return. Click on that.

4. You're just about done. Simply choose a folder on your computer's hard drive to store your soon-to-be-downloaded form. And that's it. The form will be transferred into that folder, from which you can print it out at your leisure. As you'll find, the form looks exactly like any form you'd pick up the old-fashioned way.

Bypass the IRS's attempts to be friendly and take advantage of the site's download-able forms and instructions.

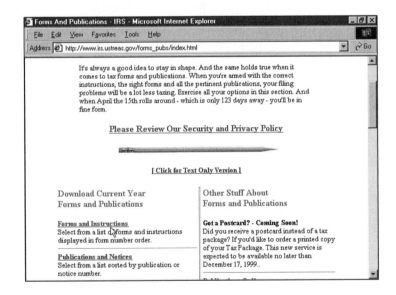

Once you have your federal forms in hand, you're halfway there. Now you just need your state forms. No problem; just about every state these days is going the same route as the IRS and making their tax forms available online. Check your state's tax department home page (which, incidentally, also tends to be a good source of tax information, especially local and regional). You can find your state's tax department home page through a search engine such as Yahoo! or Google by typing in your state's name and "taxation division" (or "taxation department," depending on how they word it in your parts). As you can see from Ohio's tax page, forms are front and center, ready for downloading. You're in business!

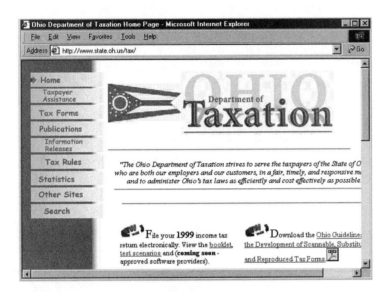

Most states have tax department information available online. The Ohio Department of Taxation's site is clean and offers what most people want up front... forms and instructions.

What Do You Owe?

Before you pay any taxes, it's often useful to know just how bad the hit is going to be. This is particularly true when capital gains taxes affect your investment portfolio. Depending on the current price of a particular stock (or some other security) and the price at which you bought it, as well as your tax rate, it might make sense to sell that investment less than 12 months after buying it and pay taxes on any increased value now. That's what we call *short-term gains*. Or, again depending on price and other market factors, it might be better to hold onto that investment longer than 12 months and postpone paying taxes, turning any future price increase into *long-term gains*. In the old days, you'd have to seek out an accountant just to get a snapshot of your capital gains picture, because it's inherently complicated and can confuse just about anyone. You should still seek professional advice when it comes to complicated tax and investment matters, but you can take care of a lot of guesswork yourself by using certain Internet tools.

For instance, take the preceding scenario. You can get a good sense of whether or not you should sell a particular investment, from a tax perspective (other market considerations should be part of your final decision-making process), by using a calculator available on Quicken's Web site. Quicken owns just about the most widely used tax software out there: TurboTax. The company has made many of TurboTax's investment decision features available for free online. Although this may be a gimmick to get you interested in buying the software, it's actually a valuable tool that you can use with no strings attached. Let's try it out. Set your browser to Quicken's tax home page at *http://www.quicken.com/taxes/.*

Quicken's Web site can show you the tax impact of a stock sale before Uncle Sam asks for his cut.

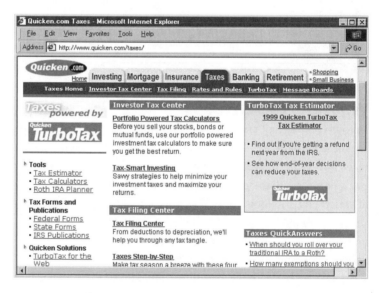

Try It Yourself ▼

1. On the menu bar at left, go to the Tools section. Select Tax Calculators.

2. You see a list of different investor decision tax calculators. Each one is presented as a question: Should you hold your shares for 12 months? What will you pay in capital gains tax? Also, the gist of the question is explained. Choose the first one, about when to sell a certain investment. This is explained as, "You can get a better after-tax return by waiting until your stocks or funds are long-term holdings; but there are still good reasons for selling early. This calculator will help you decide if you should hold or fold."

3. You now face a screen asking you to complete two steps. Under Step One, you need to tell the calculator which stock you've owned for less than 12 months. You can either click on the list at left or enter its symbol. Now move over to Step Two. Enter the number of shares you own, their purchase price and current price (the site may actually fill this in for you if it's a widely held stock and its price is readily available), and your federal tax rate. Click Calculate.

4. You immediately get your answer in the box below. Best of all, it's a detailed response, not just a couple of lines. You may be told that you can save a certain amount by making your stock a long-term holding (that is, by holding it for more than 12 months). Or you may be cautioned that if the price falls below a certain level, you're better off selling it now regardless of how long you've held it.

This is just a taste of how you can use online calculators to figure out answers to some important tax questions. You'll find a variety of other tax calculators on the Internet. Remember back in Chapter 2, when you learned about how common these online calculators are? Taxes and calculators go hand-in-hand, particularly because taxes are such nasty, confusing little things and so few of us want to sit down and try to figure them out on our own.

Remember:

As we briefly stated before, tax considerations are only part of the reason to consider selling a stock. Prevailing market conditions and other factors are important, too.

Electronic Filing

The last several years have seen the advent of electronic tax filing. You can file your federal taxes, and state taxes in many cases, via email instead of making that mad dash to the post office at midnight on April 15. You might miss the free doughnuts and coffee, the TV cameras, and the camaraderie of your fellow frantic tax-filers, but you probably won't yearn for the hassle of finding stamps or ensuring that your taxes get that all-important postmark. The online forms even use what's called an *electronic signature*, which is perfectly legitimate in the IRS's eyes.

Overheard:
The IRS claims the error rate for electronic tax returns is less than 1%, as opposed to an error rate of about 20% for paper returns.

e-Filing, as it's called, isn't for everyone. You might find it kind of nerve-racking to trust email, which has its own set of flaws, to handle something as critical as your annual income tax form. If you owe money on your taxes, you still have to arrange to send a check to the IRS. But the ranks of e-filers are expanding. In 1998, more than 24 million taxpayers used the IRS's e-file option to file their federal income tax returns, lured by the promise of faster refunds and (according to the IRS) greater accuracy.

So what's involved in e-filing? You'll find that the IRS Web site—yes, the same one you used to download forms and get general information—has extensive background information on e-filing. It's in the IRS's best interest to inform us about it; after all, processing returns electronically saves money and time. The IRS site is an authoritative source of information on this new way to file your returns.

Beware of vendors who offer to process your electronic tax return in exchange for an unreasonably steep fee—they're mushrooming all over the Internet. You need to use an authorized e-filing provider in order to transmit your tax returns to the IRS correctly, so be sure that the company you choose is authorized to perform this service. You can search the IRS's list of such providers by going to *http://www.irs.ustreas.gov/elec_svs/elf-txpyr.html*. Some of these providers will send along your electronic return for free; others will ask for a modest fee. It's worth shopping around until you find a reasonable fee from a trusted firm.

All About Audits

Worried about being audited? The very word is enough to strike terror into any self-respecting taxpayer's heart. But one site, run by Syracuse University, can help you figure out your likelihood of staring down an IRS auditor some day. You can reach it at *http://www.trac.syr.edu/tracirs*. The site includes comprehensive, nonpartisan information on the IRS, including many findings on tax code enforcement trends. It also surveys local IRS enforcement offices and their various audit rates—in other words, it can help you find out if that IRS office across town is audit-crazy or not. If you register with the site (for free), you can compare how your county stacks up against others in various tax code enforcement areas.

Still Hungry for More?

Okay, now you're up to speed on how taxes work, you have your tax forms, you're set with some basic tax approaches using calculators, and you even know whether you might want to file your returns electronically... but what about the rest of your tax picture? There's far more to tax management than filing a tax return. You need an entire tax strategy. After all, taxes affect your investments, whether you buy or sell a home, where you live, and your retirement planning.

Fortunately, in addition to general tax information, some sites offer effective consumer advocacy and counseling services aimed at solving specific problems. Some of these sites can even help you figure out your overall strategy. Check out TaxWeb at *http://www.taxweb.com*, which has answers to various tax questions and links to more detailed tax-related Web sites. This site operates as a sort of directory to other online tax resources.

If you're really getting hooked on tax information, you might even give Tax Analysts Online a whirl at *http://www.tax.org/*. This site is run by a nonprofit organization, founded in 1970, that offers publications and runs databases of tax data. It's rather scholarly, so you might be a little intimidated at first by the dry, serious approach. But if you've ever really wondered how your precious tax dollars are being spent—and we've all pondered that question at some point, usually when sighing over a tax bill—this is the site for you. Tax Analysts Online includes a page of links to federal and state organizations, such as the Multistate Tax Commission and the Federation of Tax Administrators, that can in turn tell you how all those hard-earned tax dollars of yours are being allocated. And the site's even got information on tax history—a thrilling subject if ever there was one.

In fact, taxes have infiltrated the Internet to such a degree that there's even a site directing you to other Web sites devoted to taxes. This is worth exploring if you're still hungry for more online tax information. Check out *http://www.taxsites.com* and click on whichever collection of sites tickles your fancy, ranging from software to academia.

Finding an Accountant

You shouldn't entrust your entire tax strategy to the Internet, no matter how much fun it may be to download tax forms or experiment with e-filing. This is especially true if you've experienced any major life changes in the past year, such as getting married, changing jobs, buying a house, having a baby, getting a raise, receiving a bonus, exercising stock options, or retiring, because all of those things affect your tax status. As your personal financial picture grows more complicated, you'll find that a tax professional can come in mighty handy.

So how do you find one online? As with many professionals, accountants have taken to the Internet with gusto. You can search for an accountant by trying any number of professional organizations. For instance, each state has its own CPA society, almost all of which have their own Web sites. A CPA, in case you don't know, is a certified public accountant who attains this status by passing a series of rigorous examinations and submitting to a host of ethical standards. Although a non-CPA may be perfectly qualified to counsel you on tax matters, a CPA is certain to maintain a high degree of professionalism. Tax Sites has a list of CPA societies in every state at *http://www.taxsites.com/ associations2.html#societies*. Each state's CPA society is slightly different, but many of them will have referral services for their members, in which case you can email information about the type of accounting service you need and get a list of suitable CPAs. For instance, the California Society of CPAs' site, located at *http://www.cpabsn.com/FindACPA/find.gst*, lets you search for a member based on criteria such as location and special skills.

CalCPA Online will help you find a CPA in California who's qualified to handle your unique tax situation.

A more general way to find an accountant, regardless of whether or not he or she is a CPA, is by using a search engine such as Accountant-Search at *http://www.accountant-search.com*. This service claims to list more than 100,000 accountants. You simply type in your state, city, ZIP code, and an indication of what kind of accountant you need. For instance, if you want a CPA, indicate that. You're then provided with a list of CPAs and their firms, addresses, and phone numbers. To some extent, this site doesn't go far beyond what you could do with any old Yellow Pages. Nonetheless, it does give you a list promptly and without much fuss.

On Your Way

You already knew that taxes were a big pain in the neck before you started reading this chapter, but now you've learned that the Internet can be a big help. You've seen how online resources can help you learn more about taxes and can take a lot of the legwork out of paying Uncle Sam:

- Many personal finance portals and general tax sites offer you an overview of different kinds of taxes and how they affect your financial situation.

- Federal and state tax forms alike are widely available on the Internet, although you shouldn't trust a site that's full of outdated forms.

- Electronic tax filing is becoming more popular, and many tax providers can facilitate the transmission of your tax forms to your state and federal tax offices.

- Many accountants can be located via online directories run by accounting organizations.

CHAPTER 8

Investing Online— Growing Your Nest Egg

No aspect of personal finance has been transformed as profoundly by the advent of the Internet as investing. Just a few years ago, your options for trading stocks and other investments were limited. You could either use a full-service stockbroker who'd charge you well over $100 in commissions per trade, or a discount broker who'd do it for a lot less—maybe around $45 a trade—but would provide relatively scanty support services. Today, you can use the likes of Merrill Lynch, the biggest full-service broker there is, for cheaper online trades and get the same level of services you'd have had to pay a full commission to receive several years ago. You can control pretty much every aspect of your account from the comfort of your own home.

What's more, just a few years ago few individual investors could research stocks, bonds, and mutual funds themselves. Sure, they could trot down to their library every few weeks to pore over dry phonebook-sized reports, or they could try to extrapolate what they could from *The Wall Street Journal* or an expensive investment newsletter. But in-depth investment research was beyond their reach because the Wall Street firms that conducted it and controlled it didn't make it available to anyone outside of their own customers. Thanks to the Internet, anyone with the smallest amount of investment knowledge can conduct fundamental research themselves.

And before the Internet came along, few everyday investors could find others with exactly the same investing interests. You might have thought XYZ stock was a good buy, for instance, but you couldn't find anyone else to discuss it with. Today, via dozens of chat rooms and message boards, investors all over the country can

What You'll Learn in This Chapter:

- ► How to use Web sites to learn the basics of investing.
- ► How to develop an investing strategy with mutual funds using fund-oriented Web sites.
- ► How to research stocks online.
- ► How to trade stocks and other investments using online brokerages.
- ► How to learn more about bonds via Web sites.
- ► How to responsibly use investing message boards and chat rooms.

meet and discuss stocks, bonds, and mutual funds. This phenomenon has even affected these investments' prices because the collective power of so many individuals has driven certain companies' stocks up or down.

The Investing ABCs

Learning how to invest is important. At first glance, it can be very intimidating. By nature, the world of stocks, bonds, and mutual funds sounds exclusive and clubby. The jargon is complicated. The stakes can be high—after all, unlike saving your money in the bank, investing it means that it can be lost if your investments go sour. But prudent investing is the single best way to increase your assets for the future. Time and time again, history has shown that there's no better way to grow your money over the long term than through smart long-term investing, even though you may experience some short-term pitfalls. And contrary to popular belief, investing is not just for the rich. Even with just $50 a month, you can begin investing, perhaps with a mutual fund or a couple of shares of stock.

The Internet has become an invaluable tool for educating yourself on investing because of its interactive capability and the wealth of links and other resources. Let's start by looking at a few of the sites that can teach you the basics of investing.

Chapter 2, "How Can I Use the Internet for Personal Finance?," discussed some of the educational sites out there—the so-called "university" sites that have such features as Budgeting 101. Investing is one area where these sites offer a great deal of help, precisely because investing can be so complicated. Many of these online "schools" are offered by portals with which you may be familiar by now.

Let's begin by looking at SmartMoney's site, *http://www. university.smartmoney.com*, which offers one of the best investor primers available. Although the university offers other departments besides investing, such as college planning (more on that in

Chapter 11!) and debt management, Investing 101 is a focal point for learning, offering more courses than the other areas. If you click on Investing 101 from the SmartMoney University home page, you'll come to a sort of department subdirectory showing the areas where courses are offered.

At SmartMoney's Investing 101, you'll find interactive courses to aid you in developing an investment strategy.

As with any school, this university starts with the basics that you will need to understand the rest of the course material. They're found under the first two areas, Why It Works and Risk vs. Reward. You can't start investing until you understand both its importance and the basic risk/reward gamble you're taking. No investment is ever guaranteed to increase in value, and these two areas will show you why that's true and how you can prepare yourself for those risks.

Other areas below these two will give you basic information on what a stock, bond, or mutual fund is, how it works, how you can understand fluctuating prices, and so on. For instance, let's go to a course on mutual funds.

1. Go to *http://www.university.smartmoney.com/Departments/Investing101/*.

2. Scroll down to the Mutual Funds area and click on the In This Section drop-down list to see the available courses. Click What Exactly Is a Mutual Fund? to go to that item.

3. This brings up an article explaining the ins and outs of funds. After you're finished with the first page, click on Next at the bottom and go to the following one.

4. The site automatically takes you to the next topic in the drop-down list. In this case it's Style Search, which explains how different mutual funds have varying styles or methods of investing depending on their managers, who are the professionals who run the funds. There's an interactive tool over on the right that allows you to compare the different styles' investment returns, risks, and expenses. You can find the investment objective you're interested in, such as growth, and see how it compares to other fund styles in these three areas. Go ahead—play with the Rank By drop-down list at the top of this tool and see how the positions on the chart change automatically.

5. Once you're finished, you can click Next again and move on to yet another mutual fund topic. See how the course walks you from one topic to the next? You can also leave if you're satisfied with what you've learned for now. Or, if you're not sure that mutual funds are where you want to invest but you still want to keep learning, you can move over to the left, select Stocks or Bonds, and do a similar tutorial on those topics.

▲

Once you've graduated from Investing 101, you can move on to other departments at this site, such as Taking Action and Strategic

Investing. See what we mean by "university site"? You can spend hours taking these courses, and you'll have a pretty good basic grounding in this stuff by the time you're finished. Best of all, it's free! If only *real* colleges were this affordable.

You'll find many, many investing primers like this one. It's worthwhile to spend some time in one you like before you take the plunge into investing. Get familiar with your investment objectives. For instance, are you investing for retirement? Or are you simply trying to invest for your kids' college in a few years? These factors will have a lot to do with your future investment strategy, which comes next after you've learned the basics. For example, your strategy might be rooted in mutual funds as a cornerstone, which can help diversify your risk while you pick up some valuable investing experience. Once you're more familiar with investing, you might move on to carefully and selectively buying and selling individual stocks or bonds.

Do You Like Investing? Join the Club

Millions of people who are just getting started with investing have joined investment clubs, which are groups of like-minded individuals who combine forces to invest their money. The idea is that 10 or 12 heads—or 25, or more—are better than one. Investment clubs are on the rise as the public's interest in investing takes off.

Club members usually agree on a few basic rules, such as how much money each member must contribute to the shared portfolio, how often they must put that money in, and who will manage the group's brokerage account. Usually, each club appoints a president, a treasurer, and a few other officers.

Investment clubs are easy to set up, but many people want a little extra help. After all, most clubs are set up as limited partnerships, so there are a few legal factors that come into play. So where do you turn? The National Association Investors Corporation helps investment clubs get started by offering assistance, selling specialized club software, and even hooking up members with clubs. Its Web site, *http://www.better-investing.org*, is chock-full of resources telling you why you might want to join a club, how to start one, what's new with clubs, and so on. You'll also find information on local NAIC chapters in your area.

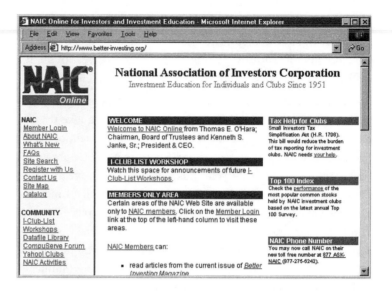

Developing an Investment Strategy with Mutual Funds

You might find it's most appropriate for you to start investing with mutual funds, which are actually portfolios of different stocks and/or bonds that are managed by professional portfolio managers on a daily basis. This gives you *diversification*, meaning that not all your eggs are in one basket, which is a key element in investing. If one stock in your fund does poorly, hopefully its losses will be cancelled out or at least diminished by other stocks that do well. Mutual funds essentially pool money from many different investments. Because of this built-in diversification, mutual funds are a good way for many beginning investors to get their feet wet. They can rest easy in the knowledge that a professional manager is keeping tabs on the portfolio each day, week, month, and quarter.

One trade-off with mutual funds, however, is that someone has to pay the manager. Every fund charges fees in some form or another to cover the cost of running the fund, advertising it to potential shareholders, and other administrative details. These fees are known as *expense ratios* and are usually represented as a number—say, 1.50. Funds with low ratios, such as those less than 1, are cheap. Those with high ratios are relatively expensive.

Expense ratios are just one aspect to consider; you might like a fund so much that you're willing to pay a little more to own it. But all expenses cut into your investment returns, so they're important to consider before you buy a particular fund. For this reason, you'll see expense ratios discussed along with fund performance at almost every step of the way when you're researching possible fund investments.

Calculating with Mutual Funds

Fortunately, the ever-present Internet calculators you've found so useful for other purposes can also help you figure out how expense ratios will come into play with mutual funds. Let's visit the Securities and Exchange Commission's site, which offers a mutual fund cost calculator to show how expenses gnaw into your returns. In case you're not familiar with the SEC, it's the federal government's main regulating body over investing. It oversees the buying and selling of all securities, whether they're funds, stocks, bonds, or other types of investments.

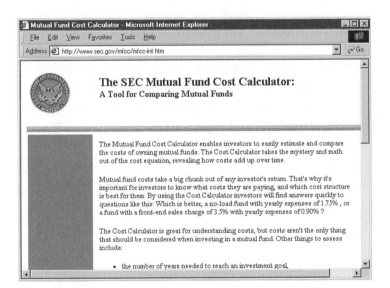

The SEC Mutual Fund Cost Calculator helps you compare the costs of owning particular mutual funds.

1. Go to *http://www.sec.gov/mfcc/mfcc-int.htm*. You'll see information here about why mutual fund expenses affect your returns. At the bottom, select whether you want to download the calculator or run it via JavaScript. Let's go with the JavaScript version.

▼ **Try It Yourself**

2. You're asked to get out your fund's prospectus because you'll need that information for the calculator. A prospectus, by the way, is a legal document that every mutual fund must provide to its shareholders. It tells you about the fund's investment style, objectives, and methods, and shows you all the relevant risks that the portfolio manager might take. It should also tell you how the fund has distributed capital gains taxes to its shareholders, how it has performed in the past (not that past performance is ever any indicator of future performance), and what sorts of expenses are associated with the fund. With your prospectus in hand, enter the appropriate information.

3. The next page explains more about why mutual fund expenses are so important. You're already an old pro at this! But read it and keep going.

4. Now you're told more about how this calculator actually arrives at its results. Again, keep going.

5. Type in how long you plan to own the fund. (We believe you should hold funds for at least 3–5 years.) If you don't know right now, just make an estimate. The longer you hold a fund, the lower your expenses are because you're essentially amortizing them over a longer time period. In other words, if you buy a fund today and sell it in three months, you've paid just as many expenses as any other shareholder, but you probably haven't had a chance to earn much on your investment in such a short time. That's a lot of expense packed into a relatively brief time span. But if you hold your fund longer, your returns will start to outpace your expenses, which are spread out more.

6. Enter your fund's expected rate of return, amount invested, expense ratio, holding period, and any sales charges. Proceed through the calculator.

7. Now you get a detailed breakdown, showing total expenses plus estimated earnings (based on expected rate of return, amount invested, expense ratios, holding period, and sales charges). This is the amount of money you'll lose by paying the expenses associated with this particular fund.

This is a good way to compare a *no-load fund* to a *load fund*, because you get an instant snapshot of how expenses affect returns. A load is a sales charge on a mutual fund that can be levied either when you buy it—that's a *front end load*—or when you sell it (a *back-end load*). Some loaded funds are excellent performers that make their sales charges well worth the expense, but some investors will avoid loads just on principle. Often, however, you'll make the decision whether or not to pay a load based on factors such as performance and fees charged. If you find two funds with similar objectives and performance, one with a load and one without, you can use a calculator such as this one to stack them against each other and see which one is more suitable for you.

Narrowing Fund Choices with Screening Engines

Choosing funds can be pretty complicated, It doesn't help that there are more than 8,000 mutual funds available. But here's where the Internet can come in extremely handy. Many investors use online screening engines, found on dozens of Web sites. How do they work? You simply enter the factors you're looking for in a fund, including the return you'd like to get and the expenses you'd be willing to pay, and you get a list of funds that meet those parameters.

Fund screening engines are found all over the Internet, but some are better than others because they're based on more extensive information and insight into the funds. One particularly good one is found at Morningstar's Web site, *http://www.morningstar.com.*

Morningstar is an organization that sells mutual fund data to individual and professional investors alike (it also provides stock research). Before you learn how its screening engines work, let's talk briefly about some of the broad fund resources available on the Morningstar site. It contains daily stories of interest to fund investors, which are particularly useful once you're up and running with a mutual fund portfolio. You'll also find free commentary from Morningstar's little army of fund analysts, who do nothing but sift through ream upon ream of fund data and spend a lot of time grilling fund managers on their investing plans.

Morningstar's army of analysts can help you evaluate more than 6,500 different mutual funds.

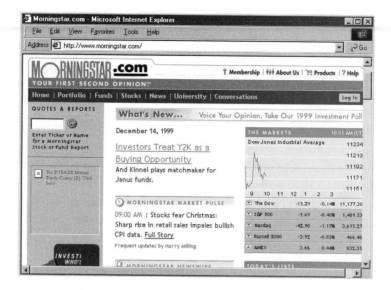

But by far the best thing about this site is the free access to the company's database of more than 6,500 mutual funds via its search engine. To use it, scroll down your screen and look over on the left, in the colored navigation bar. Under the Tool Box heading, select Fund Selector. Then select your fund category—all funds, U.S. stock funds, international funds, bond funds, or hybrid funds (which invest in both stocks and bonds)—and the investment parameters you want to use, which range from investment return to Morningstar rating to volatility. What's a Morningstar rating? That's simply a subjective system that Morningstar has developed to compare funds. Five stars is the best rating, four stars is second-best, and so on. It's a proprietary system—no company other than Morningstar can use it—that's based on a fund's returns, risk, portfolio, manager, and other factors.

After you select your parameters, you get a list of funds that have been screened for what you're looking for, along with their ticker symbols (just like stocks, funds have tickers). Be aware that Morningstar packs a lot of information into its screening engine. Although that's what makes it so good, it can be a little overwhelming at first. Indeed, if you click on any fund's ticker symbol, you get a colorful page that Morningstar calls a Quick Take report. For example, check out the Pimco Innovation Fund, which happens to be a five-star fund, at *http://quicktake.morningstar. com/Funds/Snapshot/_PIVAX.html*. As you can see, the page includes benchmarks commonly used in choosing funds, such as the growth of $10,000 invested in this fund (compared to how the same amount would do invested in the Standard & Poor's 500 index), a style box showing the kind of fund this is, and statistics such as size, return, asset allocation, the stocks or bonds held in the fund, and expense information. There's even recent news on the fund and a record of any conversations about it in the site's discussion forums. Fortunately, you can get help sifting through all this information. If you have any questions about the topics presented here, all you have to do is click on the link next to each item on the page.

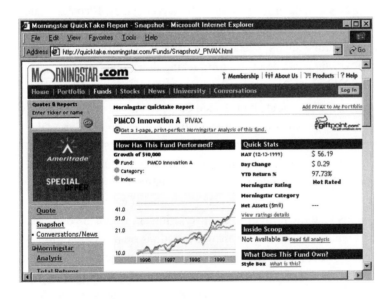

Morningstar's Quicktake Reports give you a lot of information on well-designed pages.

Searching for Duds

Not all mutual funds are created equally, that's for sure. To help you choose these investments wisely and avoid a dud along the way, many fund investors will sift through various benchmarks that establish some frame of reference for particular types of funds. Naturally, resources on the Internet have sprung up to help out with this process. Check out a site called FundAlarm at

Bits and Bytes:
Remember, though, that just because a fund has underperformed its benchmark in the past doesn't mean it can't redeem itself in the future. Last year's loser could be next year's winner if some things change, such as the manager, the characteristics of the stock market, or the investments held in the fund.

http://www.fundalarm.com, which lists so-called Three-Alarm Funds that are underperforming their respective benchmarks. These are duds that you might want to stay away from. To find the list, go to the Highlights and Commentary section of the site's home page. From there, you'll see Three-Alarm Funds under a section titled Lists. Click on it to get your dud list, along with an explanation of its methodology.

Browsing More Fund Sites

Finally, if you're still hungry for more basic fund information, you ought to check out some other basic fund sites besides Morningstar's.

One of them is the Mutual Fund Connection at *http://www.ici.org/*. This site is run by the Investment Company Institute, which is a trade group of mutual fund companies. It contains fun facts on funds and background on issues related to mutual fund law and fund shareholders' rights, as well as a directory of mutual funds, which can be useful for tracking down one fund in particular.

Another useful fund site is called Sage. It's not actually on the Internet, but rather on America Online, so you do need an AOL subscription to use it. If you do have an AOL membership, type in the keyword "Sage" to find it. In addition to useful articles and commentary on funds, Sage is most notable for its live forums with fund managers, which take place almost every day. The forums take the form of live conversations in which anyone can participate, and managers answer questions on a variety of topics, such as their investment perspectives and strategies, the economy, and so on. All of Sage's past forums are archived on the site, and you can scan through them to see which managers show up. Sage is also a useful community site in which fund investors can exchange ideas and opinions on funds.

Researching Stocks

Are you ready to take the plunge into investing in individual stocks? More and more people are, and much of this recent shift is because the Internet has made researching stocks much easier and the information more comprehensive than ever before.

Granted, the public has always had some access to stock research, usually through their stockbrokers. Investing in stocks means that you buy shares of a particular company that's public—as in, anyone can buy a piece of it. And a public company must make its financial records and results available to everyone. But finding this information used to be quite difficult, even if it was supposedly available. Shareholders were limited to whatever their company told them in its annual report—a once-a-year publication required by the SEC to be distributed to anyone who owns stock in the company—or else they could try to wade through the SEC's files or ask their broker for a research report. But it wasn't easy to research a company based on more timely factors that can influence a stock, or to compare one company to another.

Today, there are many sites that can help you sift through critically important stock information. The most common type of stock data you'll see—indeed, you'll see it on just about any financial site out there—is the stock quote. This is a snapshot of a given stock's price at a given time. In addition to stock quotes, many sites will allow you to access historical price information, analysts' ratings of a stock, and valuation tools that can help you decide if a stock is cheap or expensive relative to certain benchmarks.

Bits and Bytes:
Sound a bit confusing? Don't worry. Stock investing is a process... something you need to take one step at a time. You'll probably want to refer back to the same so-called university Web sites you used earlier in this chapter.

You can also learn about stocks and stock research by visiting some good general sites. One such site is the SEC's Office of Investor Education and Advice at *http://www.sec.gov/oiea1.htm*. Once you get past the stiff-sounding bureaucratic name, it's actually a surprisingly refreshing site packed with good information. For example, there are detailed instructions on how to use Edgar, the SEC's database of corporate filings (which are the financial reports that all public companies are required to share with the government every three months and in certain other situations). You can even find out if that old stock certificate in your attic is worth anything—a surprisingly common question for many of us. Who knows? You could get lucky. The SEC site also has practical tips on what to do if a company in which you own stock ceases operations or files for bankruptcy.

Armed with a primer on stock investing, you might feel ready to buy shares of a stock or two. But don't take that leap until you've got at least some minimal research under your belt.

Applying Internet Research Tools

Let's take a look at a stock research tool on the Internet that teaches you the basics of stock research as you're getting real information on stocks. It's MSN MoneyCentral's Research Wizard tool, located at *http://moneycentral.msn.com/investor/research/wizards/SRW.asp*.

A number of sites, such as MoneyCentral, offer research wizards.

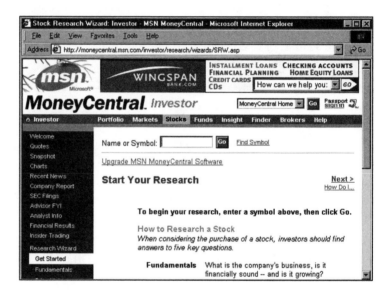

Research Wizard starts by walking you through the five key aspects of any stock:

Fundamentals	What's the company's business, and is it fiscally sound?
Price History	How much have other investors been willing to pay for a share over a period of time?
Price Target	What do analysts think of the stock's price appreciation potential?
Catalysts	What catalysts will affect how investors feel about the stock?
Comparison	How does this stock compare to others, both its peers in this industry and others completely unrelated to it?

These are some of the same factors that professional stock analysts review when they look at a stock.

As you look at these research criteria, Research Wizard will explain what each data point means. Start by entering a stock symbol at the top. You immediately get a page full of that stock's fundamentals, the building blocks of your research. This will include easy-to-understand information on how much the company earns, how fast it's growing, how profitable it is, and so forth.

By the time you get to the details on which events may affect your stock, some real value kicks in. The site gives you links to your stock's recent news, SEC filings, and other legal filings. When you get to the Comparison page, you can enter another stock symbol to see how it stacks up against your original pick. Or you can display all the companies in your first stock's industry, which can help you benchmark your stock against its peers. This is useful because all the companies in a given industry face similar challenges. If oil prices are low, for instance, all gas refinery companies must struggle harder to make profits regardless of their own individual strategies.

Above all, the best thing about Research Wizard is its simple, straightforward language, free of the jargon that can make stock research such a chore sometimes. This site just comes out and asks the questions in plain English:

- Whose share price is likely to gain the most?

- Who sold and earned the most over the past 12 months?

- Whose financial health is strongest?

You get the idea.

Okay, so you've done some basic research. Think you're ready to buy? Not so fast. You still have some work ahead of you. Good stock research takes current events into account as well. News can have amazing impact on a stock's price, which of course drives performance and, ultimately, your investment returns.

Exploring Financial News Sites

There are many, many useful financial news sites on the Internet.
So many, in fact, that you'll find them rather difficult to tell apart
because many contain similar information: the day's news,
updated statistics throughout the day showing the stock market's
performance, and usually a search engine with which you can pull
up a quote on any given stock.

But one particularly good news site is CNBC at *http://www.
cnbc.com*. It has a ticker at the bottom of the home page, which
gives you a quick glance at stock prices as they glide by—you
might appreciate this more as you develop a stock portfolio. It
also puts the major stock indexes' performance (the S&P 500, for
instance) front and center. If you just have a few moments during
your day to check financial news, this is a good site to bookmark.
All the financial news you need is on this site.

*CNBC.com is a
good site to book-
mark because of
its extensive cov-
erage of the
market.*

Another useful site is CBS MarketWatch at *http://www.cbs.
marketwatch.com*. It's slightly less cluttered than CNBC.com. To
a new stock investor, this can be a little less intimidating. Also,
you can search for news about a particular stock by clicking Find
Your News.

Just the Facts

Sometimes all you really want to know about a stock is the barest of bare-bones information: what it does, where it's based, its address, and so on. A good source for such basic, straight-up data is Hoover's Online at *http://www.hoovers.com*. Hoover's has been published for years in book form, and was usually just available in libraries. But now much of this information is available free of charge on the Internet. This material is factual, unbiased data on companies' business objectives, locations, officers, size, and so on. Hoover's still charges a fee for some information—indicated by a little gold key next to the link—but much of what you need is accessible at absolutely no cost.

Trading Online

You've learned how stocks work. You've done your research. Now you're ready to take the plunge and actually buy a stock or two. If you choose to make this transaction online, as millions of people do, you have plenty of resources from which to choose. The last couple of years have seen an explosion in the number of online trading firms. Some of them offer trades for as little as $8 each!

But don't choose your online brokerage firm based on price alone. You want to look for a firm that meets a whole set of important criteria—how well it executes trades, for instance. Can it ensure that your request to buy or sell a particular stock at a particular price is actually executed? How well does it provide information about your account? Can you email a customer service rep if you need to? Perhaps most importantly, how good are its support services if its online trading capabilities suddenly fail? You've probably heard about online trading sites that have gone down unexpectedly on a busy stock market afternoon, leaving thousands of customers stranded with no way to trade their stocks.

Fortunately, you can determine the best online trading firm by using a site you've already visited. In Chapter 4, "Banking Online—Managing Your Money over the Internet," you looked at reviews of Internet banks by Gomez Advisors, a well-respected independent consulting firm. Their site is even more widely known as a rating service for online stock brokerages. To check

Bits and Bytes:

Gomez advisors, an excellent brokerage rating sevice, has released a list of the top online brokerage firms. The following were rated as the best in overall sevice:

1. Charles Schwab (*www. schwab.com*)

2. E*Trade (*www. etrade.com*)

3. DLJdirect (*www.dljdirect. com*)

You can see the complete list at *www.gomez.com*.

out a brokerage, just go to Gomez's home page, *http://www.gomezadvisors.com*, and choose Brokers under the Personal Finance section. You'll find a list of brokers ranked according to a variety of important criteria, and you can search and mix criteria according to what's most important to you.

No two online brokerages are the same, even though they have similar functions. Indeed, these firms try hard to differentiate themselves because they all essentially offer the same service. But let's look at one typical online firm just to get a feel for its capabilities and specific services. Let's walk through Ameritrade, one of the larger online brokerage firms.

Ameritrade's demo lets you see what it would be like to place a trade on their system.

Try It Yourself ▼

1. Go to *http://www.ameritrade.com*. You see a big promo for Ameritrade's famed $8 trades, an invitation to open an account, and a few other buttons. Choose the one marked Learn More.

2. This brings up a list of Ameritrade's advantages—or at least what their marketing department says are the advantages (decide for yourself). Skip this list and move over to the yellow navigation bar on the left. Click on the third item down, Internet Demo.

3. This is a trading demonstration designed to show you how online trades work. Read the introduction and then click Next.

4. Now you're shown how Ameritrade gives you quotes on stocks you're considering buying or selling. Enter the ticker symbol. You get a fairly impressive set of data called an Extended Quote, which actually goes beyond simple stock prices to show you some fundamentals of the stock. If you're ready to place an order for a stock, scroll down to the bottom and click the Equity Orders arrow. (Equity is a fancy term for stock.)

5. Now you're looking at Ameritrade's basic trading page. You're given a choice of buying or selling a stock, as well as the number of shares you want to trade, and there's a place to enter the symbol for that stock. You also need to decide if you want to place a market order or a limit order. Choose a limit order.

6. Because you've chosen a limit order, you must now specify your limits—that is, the maximum you want to pay, or *bid*, for these shares. When you're finished entering this information, click the Preview Order button.

7. The next screen summarizes your order. (This is just a demo, so it inserts a hypothetical stock for you.) This summary includes a refresher of the stock's current price and a few other details. Review it and click on the button marked Place Order.

8. You're done—or at least you would be if this were a real trade. This screen shows your trade and gives you an order number so you can track it if it's delayed in processing or you have some other questions down the line. You're also offered the opportunity to review the order again, along with all the other orders you may have placed in the past 60 days.

Now, online trading isn't for everyone. Some of us will never feel truly comfortable making a transaction that may involve thousands of dollars by tapping a few keys. You may find that trading online is a bit *too* easy. You may take unnecessary risks because it's so cheap and fast to zap in a few trades. Of course, this can lead to financial problems down the line. But online trading has opened up the world of stocks to millions of people who might otherwise limit their investing activity to mutual funds, or might not even invest at all. Do it very carefully, take it one step at a time, and it can be extremely rewarding—even fun.

Exploring Bonds

Mutual funds and stocks might get more attention than bonds, but don't overlook them. Bonds represent money owed by the entity that issues them. When you buy a bond, you're acting as a creditor to the bond issuer. For instance, let's say the city of Chicago issues municipal bonds in order to raise money for a new football stadium. It promises to repay that money to the bondholders by a certain date, which is the bond's maturity date, plus interest. That interest, as well as the guarantee that the bond's face value will be repaid at maturity, is what attracts the bond buyer. Investment grade bonds rated AAA are among the safest and most conservative of all bond investments.

You can buy and sell bonds online in much the same way as you do stocks, and you can research them much the same way as well. But bonds are a different animal indeed. It's well worth your time to learn more about how they work, how they're priced, and how to interpret the different bond ratings you'll hear about (bonds are rated from AAA, the best, to C and below, representing different degrees of risk).

A good Web site for this purpose, *http://www.investinginbonds. com*, is sponsored by the Bond Market Association, a trade group for bond issuers. The site offers basic information on bonds, as well as an investor's checklist with which you can determine if bonds are a suitable investment for your objectives. Generally, the older you are, the more appropriate highly rated bonds are for your portfolio because they pose less risk overall than many other investments, particularly stocks. If you're that much closer to retirement, you stand to lose less of your assets if the stock market hits a rough spot. If you're younger, however, you might decide that bonds should make up a relatively small portion of your investment portfolio. Determining which portion of your portfolio should be bonds and which should be stocks (not to mention other types of investments and even cash) is called *asset allocation.*

For more information on asset allocation, see Chapter 12, "Retirement—Planning and Financing Your Golden Years."

Investing Message Boards and Chat Rooms

What would investing on the Internet be without message boards and chat rooms? As mentioned at the beginning of this chapter, the Internet's capability to foster communication between investors everywhere has helped revolutionize investing.

As you probably know, online message boards are forums where people can post thoughts and opinions for others to read and discuss. Chat rooms are live virtual conversation spaces with people who might be thousands of miles away from each other. Because there's so much to talk about when it comes to investing—such as which mutual funds are doing well, which stock might hit gold next, and so on—message boards and chat rooms go hand-in-hand with investing. All investors have opinions, and these forums give them a chance to share.

You shouldn't let message boards and chat rooms supplant your own diligent stock research or make your investing decisions for you (remember, people's opinions are not always based on fact, and they can be wrong or even inflammatory). But these forums add a great deal of color, liveliness, and even valuable information to the investing process.

Bits and Bytes: As long as you take investing chat rooms with a few big grains of salt, they're worth visiting.

Try several message boards and see which ones you like. You'll see them on many sites, including financial portals, certain online brokerages, and even some financial news sites. Other sites devote themselves almost entirely to running myriad message boards and let their other content, such as news or stock quotes, come second. One of these is Raging Bull at *http://www.ragingbull.com.* This site runs dozens and dozens of boards on various stocks and investing topics. On its home page, the site summarizes the most compelling opinions expressed by its members. There's even a bar graph, updated hourly, showing the day's most active message boards. Again, you shouldn't let a message board sway your investing decisions, but sites such as Raging Bull do provide a sense of community. And with millions of animated and excited members, they're certainly entertaining. However, a lot of bad information appears on message boards and in chat rooms.

Raging Bull hosts lots of investing chat rooms and message boards— an investor's vox populi.

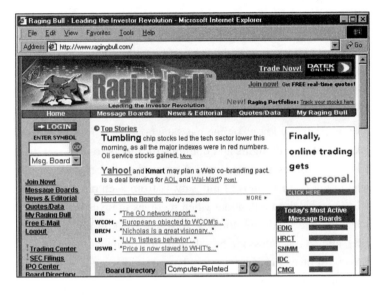

On Your Way

You're already aware that the Internet and investing are like two peas in a pod—few elements of personal finance have adapted so well to this environment. In fact, it seems as if the investing world was just waiting for something like the Internet to come along and make investing so much more accessible to so many millions of people.

- Investing results are never guaranteed, but investing is the best way to maximize your assets for the future. Many Web sites teach you the basics of investing safely and with minimal risk.

- Mutual funds are ideal for beginning investors because they help diversify risk. However, you need to keep an eye on fund expenses.

- Research is a critical part of investing in stocks, and the Internet is well adapted to provide a host of research tools. Many of these tools are the same ones that professional stock analysts use.

- Investing online not only saves you money in commissions, but it's relatively easy and efficient provided you find a firm you feel comfortable with.

- Investment grade bonds are another way to diversify your investments and generally pose less risk than common stocks.

- Community message boards and chat rooms allow investors all over the world to discuss investing topics, and they can add a lot of color and excitement to the process... but beware.

PART IV

Meeting Goals
Along the Way

CHAPTER 9

Family Finances—Your Changing Needs as Your Family Grows

If you've ever done a household budget (you haven't?), bought life insurance, or given some thought to saving and investing money for the future, you've already dabbled in family finance. It touches on just about every aspect of personal finance, because—like it or not—everything about starting and running a family comes back to money. From getting married (paying for that big wedding) to having that first baby (have you checked how much diapers and formula cost lately, not to mention day care and college?) to buying a minivan as your family expands (no, the hatchback won't cut it anymore), to planning the annual family vacation (airfare for four... yikes!), it all involves money.

How can the Internet help you with your family finances? There are many sites that provide a basic education on the subject, as well as calculators that can help you figure out how to keep your growing family's expenses in line. Some of these sites are actually sponsored by companies that sell family-oriented financial products, so you'll need to be a little wary of them even as you enjoy their contents. Others are more general family sites—such as those that focus on parenting—most of which include financial components. Still others are the personal finance portals that you're probably quite familiar with by now.

No matter what kind of site you use, you'll thank yourself for exploring this aspect of finance online. Chances are that using the Internet to help you manage your family's finances will help you save time—and time is among any family's most precious resources.

On that note, let's get started!

What You'll Learn in This Chapter:

▶ How to find general family personal finance information on various Web sites.

▶ How to start family financial planning before you even say "I do."

▶ How Web sites may assist you in figuring out a budget for a new baby as well as other challenges of your growing family.

▶ How to educate your kids about money matters (need a little help yourself?).

▶ How to approach single parenthood from a financial perspective.

Figuring Out Family Finance

If money touches on just about every aspect of running a family today, where on earth should you begin to learn about family finance? It's a broad topic, indeed. Several sites offer a good introduction to the many facets of family finance.

One of these sites is actually run by a vendor of services, as hinted at in this chapter's introduction. Yes, yes, it's trying to sell you something, but you can actually derive quite a bit of value from this site even though you might see a sales pitch or two creep onto your screen. Just remember whose site it is and it shouldn't be too hard to ignore the pitches (unless that's what brought you there in the first place). We're talking about Metropolitan Life Insurance's LifeAdvice Library, part of the company's main Web site at *http://www.metlife.com/*.

You'll find a wide range of friendly articles here on various subjects, such as choosing a summer camp, figuring out if your elderly relative might need to make better financial arrangements, becoming a grandparent for the first time, and so on. As you know, all of this material is intertwined with financial issues, so it's helpful to start thinking about how to address such life events from a money perspective. The best thing about LifeAdvice Library, in fact, is that it has links to miscellaneous calculators and other online resources so you can figure it out for yourself. The links you choose will depend on which of these life events interest you, of course, but there's something here for practically everyone.

Another site that offers a general glimpse into family finance is *http://www.loveathome.com/*. This isn't a financial site per se. In fact, Love At Home is a parenting and family site that happens to have financial content. But because the site itself goes in such broad directions, the articles it publishes on finance tend to be very helpful with general family money issues. You'd find Love At Home's financial pieces on the left side, in the grayish navigation bar. Under Columns, there's a listing for Family Finance. The site contains columns that, like Met Life's LifeAdvice Library, run the gamut of family financial topics. You can check the site's archives at the top of the home page for articles that you've missed.

As you're starting to see, educational background articles on family finance can pop up in some pretty diverse places. You might try to find more of them—new articles come out far more frequently than we can keep track of—by using a conventional search engine's family finance section. Check out Excite.com's Family Finance search page at *http://www.excite.com/family/ family_planning/family_finance/*. You immediately get a list of relevant sites. The page also offers you access to message boards on family finance. It's up to you to figure out which aspect of family finance you want to explore first—is it figuring out how much summer camp might cost, for example, or getting a handle on your kids' allowances? Again, don't be surprised to find Web sites that, on the surface, might seem to have relatively little to do with money. Family finance can take you in some pretty far-ranging directions.

Excite's Family Finance page has links to other resources.

Financial Planning Right from the Start

So, you're engaged! You and your new spouse-to-be are indeed a new family, even if it's just the two of you. Now is the time to start forming good family financial habits so you're not scrambling for a strategy when your family grows.

In most cases, getting married is a financial event unto itself. Unless you're planning on a small "justice of the peace" type of wedding or some impromptu Las Vegas nuptials, chances are you're going to spend about $20,000 or so before the wedding day is over. Of course, your wedding could cost far more depending on where you live, how many people you invite, and even the day of the week and time of year you get married.

Before you start writing checks to DJs and bridal shops, however, you and your betrothed ought to sit down and discuss your respective approaches to money. You're in love, of course, and you're ready to spend the rest of your lives together, but do you really know if you have the same views on financial matters? No? Well, you should—again, money touches on just about every facet of both of your lifestyles.

Fortunately, there are Web sites that address these issues. One of them is iVillage, which has an entire section on financial matters called MoneyLife. Within MoneyLife is a subsection called Love & Money, which—you guessed it—helps couples figure out the role of money in their relationships. Check out the columns by going to *http://www.ivillagemoneylife.com* and choosing the heading Love & Money from the amber-colored navigation bar on the left (it's the eighth item down from the top under Features). You'll get a list of articles on this topic, ranging from "Love Me and My $$ Issues" to "My Partner Overspends!" Ample fodder for some pleasant candlelit dinner conversations, right?

Overheard:
You don't have to be Donald Trump or Bill Gates to want—or need—a prenuptial agreement. Sometimes, they can be smart financial planning tools. Get the basics on prenups by going to *http://www.bankrate. com/brm/prenup.asp.*

Regardless of where you discuss these issues, you should take some action now. You can start by taking iVillage's Money Styles quiz at *http://www.ivillagemoneylife.com/money/quiz/ 0,4055,12471~356,00.html.* It's a fun way to see how you and your future wife or husband approach money.

When it comes to budgeting for the wedding itself, the Internet is no slouch either. You might want to check out a variety of specialized wedding sites. There's a wedding budget calculator at *http://www.theknot.com* that will help you figure out how to pay for all those table centerpieces and party favors. At *http://www.infostuff.com/weddings*, you'll see a heading called Budget that gives you an idea of where your money tends to go when you're planning and paying for a typical wedding.

As Your Family Grows

Your first baby is likely to catch you off guard—you won't be prepared for getting so little sleep, and you might be surprised at how Baby changes your lifestyle. But don't get caught by surprise when it comes to the financial picture.

Did you ever think about how much babies cost? By the time Baby heads off to college, you'll have spent hundreds of thousands of dollars on everything from formula to football cleats. Fortunately, it doesn't all hit at once. That big expense is amortized over a number of years, so you have ample time to figure out how you'll cover your costs. Many Web sites offer budgeting tools that can assist you in this process. Some of them are so similar to the budgeting sites discussed back in Chapter 3, "Budgeting—Planning for Today and the Future," that it doesn't make much sense to go over them again. But others are quite different.

For more information on budgeting tools, see Chapter 3.

You'll find a lot of budgeting assistance on general parenting sites, which often devote big chunks of their space to financial topics because money plays such a huge role in raising a family. Some of them take the form of calculators that let you determine just how much money to set aside in your monthly budget for your new baby, depending on your lifestyle. Let's visit *http://www.babycenter.com*, which focuses mostly on parenting young children.

1. From the site's home page, choose the heading marked Baby on the left side of the navigation bar. It's the fourth item down.

2. You're presented with a table of contents. In the column on the right, about halfway down, is an item called Family Finances. Click on that link.

3. You now have a rather long list of personal finance articles to choose from. Scroll down and click the Budgeting for Baby link.

▼ **Try It Yourself**

4. Now you have a page called Cost of Baby, sponsored by a vendor, American Century Investments, in cooperation with the BabyCenter site. Don't worry that it's vendor-sponsored. The information is still useful, and it's easy to ignore a sales pitch if you know it's there. Read the instructions for the calculator, which is on this same page. Then start filling in answers to the questions. As you can see, this calculator helps you determine how much you'll spend on your child based on your lifestyle. When you're finished, just click Calculate at the bottom.

5. Here's the bottom line! The calculator gives you a rough estimate of what you can expect to spend by the time Baby hits the age of 18. It also goes into some detail about what you'll spend during various phases of childhood (such as birth to age one, age one to four years, and so on), and it tells you how you'll be spending all that money during those phases.

Having a child means recalculating your financial plans, and BabyCenter.com has a very useful calculator.

You'll find a range of other articles on BabyCenter's site that will help you assess how Baby's entry into the family will affect your bottom line. It's worth surfing around in that list of articles from Step 3.

For more help with assessing the financial impact of a new baby on your family and making sure your financial planning keeps pace, you might want to go back to iVillage's site. Remember the MoneyLife section that offered help before you even got married? The same site delves quite a bit into the subject of how kids affect your family budget. You have to work at finding this section—unfortunately, it's several mouse clicks from the site's home page—but it's worth it once you do. For a shortcut, go to *http://www.ivillagemoneylife.com/money/life_stage/coupleskids/*. You'll find a virtual shelf full of articles by columnist Jill Gianola, a financial planner from Ohio. She covers everything from dealing with stepchildren from a financial perspective to home budgeting to how to talk to your kids about money issues. Don't be afraid to explore this site in greater detail. You never know where you might find some useful family financial information. For instance, the iVillage site's Couples and Kids area has its own message boards on creating and managing budgets and saving money.

Teaching kids about money is indeed valuable, not to mention necessary. These days children are exposed to money pressures earlier than ever—you've probably heard of high school kids getting credit card solicitations, for instance. Many parents give their children credit cards to use in emergencies. Some children even start investing at a young age with money given to them by their grandparents or other relatives. But does your kid know the *real* meaning of money? How does she handle her allowance? Will she get a job before she graduates from high school? And if so, how will she handle the money she earns? At what age does she need her first bank account? All of these questions must be answered at some point—preferably before your child faces her first big financial decision.

A good Internet resource on this topic is Family Money's site at *http://www.familymoney.com*. On the home page, you'll see a heading called Family Finances in the left-hand navigation bar. Under that heading is a link called Kids & Money that contains a variety of articles on the subject, including nuts-and-bolts pieces on walking your children through money issues, teaching them to be consumers, and managing allowances. There's even a list of books you can encourage your kids to read so they can learn more about money on their own. You'll also find a question-and-answer column.

Family Money is a good site that offers general advice on a wide variety of topics.

Suddenly Single

Things don't always go as planned in life, and at some point, whether by choice or not, you might find yourself raising a family without a spouse. One-third of American households have a single parent. In many cases, this situation poses some extra financial challenges. For example, how much you need to spend on your day-to-day family responsibilities affects how much money you can save for retirement, or for a home. If you're a single parent, those effects can be even more dramatic. But regardless of your financial situation today, you need to think about the big picture. You may be struggling to make ends meet on one salary, but you'll still need to plan your retirement.

So how do you do it? It's not easy, but there are numerous Internet resources to help you.

Suppose you've just been divorced. In addition to single parent-hood, you may also be paying child support and alimony, manag-ing your family's finances more directly than before, and so on. You're hardly alone. You'll encounter quite a few divorce-oriented Web sites that are stocked with information on the financial con-sequences of this life change. One of them is *http://www.divorcesource.com*. A big chunk of the site is community-oriented, built around message boards that let you exchange ideas with fellow divorced people. Over on the amber-colored naviga-tion bar to the left, scroll down to see a heading called Message Centers. Under it, you'll see a listing titled Financial. These boards are big, so be prepared to wade through possibly hundreds of messages, but you'll find some good information and cama-raderie.

More helpful are the site's articles and interactive worksheets on financial issues, which you'll find at *http://www.divorcesource.com/archives/financial.shtml*. These articles have been submitted by attorneys who work with the DivorceSource Web site, so they may have links back to certain law firms or other legal sites. Don't worry about that. Just read the information for what it is: good background.

Divorce isn't the only way you might become a single parent. People who've suffered the death of a spouse deal with their own set of issues as financial needs and priorities become clouded with grief. For them there's *http://www.ka-ching.com*, a personal finance Web site that talks about many aspects of money, not just this one. (It happens to be aimed chiefly at women, although any-one can use its information.) Ka-ching is one of the few sites that addresses the financial impact of losing one's spouse. You'll have to search for a little while to reach these articles, but they're worth finding. Start at the section marked Your Family right at the center of the home page. On the next page, click on the heading labeled As a Partner. Under Basics, you'll see links to several arti-cles on this subject.

Believe it or not, you'll also find some useful resources on single parenthood back at iVillage's site. The MoneyLife section, which you may have already visited for information on marriage and

talking to your kids about money, also has a subsection titled
Suddenly Single. As you'd expect, the articles here address child
support issues, separating your finances from your former
spouse's, flextime issues with employers, child care costs, divorce
settlement, and so on. They're written by *USA Today* columnist
Kerry Hannon, who's an expert on these matters—she has also
written an excellent book titled *Suddenly Single: Money Skills for
Divorcees and Widows* that is well worth purchasing.

On Your Way

Money and families are difficult to separate. As your family
grows and changes, money issues will undoubtedly change too.
But you can use the Internet to help you manage a wide variety of
family money issues.

- Many Web sites that appear to have little to do with personal
  finance topics are, in fact, gold mines of information about
  family finance.

- Family financial planning starts before you even get married.
  It's worthwhile to hash out some issues with your prospective
  spouse before marching down the aisle.

- A new baby brings many changes, not the least of which are
  financial, and there are online tools that can help you assess
  how raising Baby will affect your family's finances.

- Single parenthood brings its own set of financial challenges.
  You should explore a variety of Web sites.

CHAPTER 10

Real Estate—Buying and Selling Online

So you're ready to buy a house—or maybe sell your current one and move up or down to a new one. But before you start picking out wallpaper or tagging stuff for a garage sale, log on to the Internet. There's an abundance of information online to help you with just about every facet of buying and selling a home. Some of it is so useful, it might make you wonder how anyone bought or sold real estate before the Internet came along.

This chapter will look at the most important parts of buying or selling a house, which are the biggest financial transactions most of us will ever make—not to mention among the most nerve-racking and emotional.

The Internet's home resources are helpful even before you've found a home. There are sites that can help you figure out where to live and how much you should plan to spend on a new home. Once you have a sense of where you're looking and whether you should be eyeing eight-bedroom villas or two-bedroom condos, a number of sites will guide you to exactly the right property in your area, your price range, and so on. If you're selling your home and need to find a real estate agent, there are sites that will put you in touch with one in your area.

When you get down to the real nitty-gritty of home buying and selling—all that negotiating, fine print, credit report scrutiny, and so on—a number of sites will help you find a mortgage. Some will even let you apply online. (Hey, anytime you can avoid sitting across a desk from some stone-faced mortgage guy, that's a plus.) You might not need to set foot in a lender's office until you sign the final papers for your loan.

What You'll Learn in This Chapter:

- ▶ How to differentiate between home-buying sites that are purely informational and those that are trying to sell you a product or service.
- ▶ How to use a mortgage calculator to figure out how much money you can afford to spend on your new home.
- ▶ How to compare mortgage interest rates online.
- ▶ How to apply for a mortgage online.
- ▶ How to view homes for purchase on the Internet.
- ▶ How to find related services such as relocation advisors that can help you with the home-buying process.

This chapter will also look at Web sites where you can find people to help close your real estate deal, which is one of the trickiest and most nail-biting parts of the whole process. If you're buying, you need an inspector to look over your future dream house. Whether you're buying or selling, you'll need an attorney. We'll show you how to find one using Internet resources.

So let's get going. Your dream home awaits you!

There's a Sales Pitch in the Air

Caveat emptor!! You probably learned this lesson way back in grade school when you blew your allowance on something you instantly regretted buying, but it bears repeating because many of the sites in the real estate field are trying to sell you something.

A critical fault line runs down the landscape of real estate sites. On one side, you have your objective, unbiased sites that simply provide information. They might feature ads on their pages and aren't exactly running the sites for charity (and why should they?), but they're not necessarily pushing a particular product either. On the other side, you'll find sites that are promoting particular mortgage brands over others (you'll often see them referred to as "preferred" or "selected" brands), certain real estate agencies, and the like. Beware of their agenda! The name of the game is not to be sold—unless, of course, you *want* to be.

So why even bother discussing these "sales-y" sites? Because they can be useful when you're shopping around for that zero-point, low-interest mortgage and you want to compare specific lenders; or when Realtor Suzy doesn't have nearly as many listings in your area as Realtor Sally. You get the idea. Unfortunately, some sites are a bit of both kinds. They might *seem* unbiased, and much of the information they contain is objective, but they also list vendors and service organizations that have probably paid a fee for that privilege.

Another point to remember: Buying and selling a home completely online is possible, but it's probably unwise unless you've been wheeling and dealing in real estate for years and your name is Donald Trump (in which case you probably have an army of underlings to lock in your interest rate and find your broker). If this is the first property you've bought or sold—or even the second or third—don't let the Internet replace good old face-to-face interaction with your real estate agent and attorney. Although some people have bought houses they've only ever seen on their Web browser, you're much better off checking out your dream house in person. Besides, it's more fun that way.

That said, the Internet can give you a great head start on all of these home matters.

So Where Do You Want To Live?

America is full of wanderers. There's a lot to be said for sticking around where you grew up, but let's face it—not too many of us actually do nowadays. As a nation, we like to hit the road in search of our fortunes. If you're especially mobile, you may already be on your second or third city or state, or even thousands of miles from your childhood home. Relocating yet again is always an option, particularly if your job demands it.

But where do you go? Sometimes you don't have much choice, as with job-related moves. Other times, the road could lead anywhere. Let's look at some sites that can help you with the sometimes bewildering process of relocating.

These sites are comprehensive guides to relocating, full of links to everything from local moving companies to mortgage banks to daycare providers in a given city. These can be gold mines of information, but they take a little getting used to because they contain so much information. They're like warehouses of relocation data, with many links to other sites that can help you with job searches, moving, and so on. You're best off using them for their voluminous data on particular towns or states that you might be considering for your new home.

One such guide is *http://www.relocationcentral.com*, which is most useful for its search feature. With it you can get detailed current information about a given city and its cost of living, jobs, taxes, and so on. Let's say you're pondering a big move to… oh, Maryland. Click the State Selector link, choose Maryland, and you get detailed information on the state's climate, population, unemployment rate, largest employers (along with their own site links, addresses, and phone numbers), government, crime rates, education, and tax scales. There's even a list of the state's members of Congress. That's more than you might know about where you live now!

Talk about too much information... At Relocation Central, you can even find your final resting place.

Interested in finding your final resting place in Maryland? The site links to Find-A-Grave: Maryland. Want some sense of history and tradition? You can link to a virtual tour of Maryland's capital, Annapolis. This Web site enables you to access this information for all states except, for some reason, North Dakota, Maine, Alaska, and Hawaii. Go figure.

Now go back to Relocation Central's home page and click on Products and Services. This is what we call information overload. Unless you already know what you want, you'll be navigating through this section for hours. Many of the links are simply vendors of services, such as mortgage companies and insurance agents, although some of this information is very helpful.

You can do just about all the same things at *http://www. virtualrelocation.com*, which is very similar to the Relocation Central site. But Virtual Relocation has another nifty feature that allows you to run detailed comparisons between two towns. Let's say you want to compare all those critical lifestyle items—cost of living, taxes, job growth, and so on—between the city you live in now and the one you're considering. Virtual Relocation's City Comparison feature will give you a detailed side-by-side explanation of data for each city.

1. Go to Virtual Relocation's home page. Under Features on the left, click on City Comparison.

▼ **Try It Yourself**

2. You get two scrollbars, one for the state where you live now and the other for the state you're thinking of moving to. The site calls it your destination state. Scroll down, highlight the two states, and click on Next at the bottom.

3. There are two similar scrollbars for the cities and towns tracked by Virtual Relocation. Unfortunately, the site doesn't cover smaller towns or villages, but if your heart is set on a tiny burg, just choose the town nearest to it. As you did before, scroll down and highlight each town. Then click on Compare Cities at the bottom.

4. Now you're in business. You get a clear comparison chart, showing your home city on the left and your future home on the right. In this example, you're comparing Chapel Hill, NC, with Little Rock, AR. See how the site stacks up cost of living, tax rates, job growth, unemployment, housing costs, and even electricity bills and ozone levels? Pretty amazing.

▲

Virtual Relocation lets you compare two cities right down to utility bills and ozone levels.

Other Web sites might have so-called salary calculators, which tell you how much money you need to make in a given city to maintain the standard of living you have now, but Virtual Relocation's City Comparisons feature goes much further. You can compare your daily costs—such as the electric bill—rather than just overall salary differences.

Talk to the Experts

You can compare cities to your heart's content, but what do the experts say? Every year *Money* magazine ranks cities according to various factors, such as cost of living, cultural and recreational activities, crime rates, education, and more. Now the magazine is putting these lists on the Internet and adding interactive features that make it even easier to pick your future home.

You can find *Money's* annual city ratings at *http://www.pathfinder.com/ money/depts/real_estate/bestplaces/*. Winners are divided into big cities and small towns (although *Money's* idea of a small town includes the likes of Boulder, Colorado, which doesn't exactly seem like Podunk to us). Along with the same article that appears in the regular *Money* magazine is a screening tool that lets you plug in the characteristics of a town that most appeal to you—pretty cool, considering that not all of us agree with a bunch of magazine editors back in New York City. But the screening tool is actually quite complicated, so you might not want to use it unless you plan on spending some serious time with this site. To see which cities scored highest in the weather category, for example, you need to pore over 15 different weather factors ranging from altitude above sea level to earthquake risk, assigning how important each factor is to you.

How Much Can You Spend?

Now that you have a better sense of where you want to live, you've got to figure out how much you can lay out for that house. Of course, that depends on many factors, including your household income, debt, credit history, savings, and interest rates. But the most important factors that affect the size of the mortgage for which you may qualify are your income (how much comes in every month), your debt (how much goes out), and how large a down payment you'll be able to scrape together.

That's where the Internet comes in handy. It's full of useful calculators that can help you figure out how much you can afford.

These calculators are practically a dime a dozen; in fact, you'll see them on objective personal finance Web sites, but they're also popping up on mortgage lenders' Web sites along with the sales pitches. Don't worry too much about using a mortgage calculator from a lender's site—it won't lock you into anything or make you buy something.

Let's compare two calculators, one from Homefair.com, a relatively unbiased provider of home-buying information, and one from Countrywide Home Loans, one of the nation's biggest mortgage banks.

Go to *http://www.homefair.com/usr/qualcalcform.html* and type in the information you're asked to give. This information is boiled down to the essentials: your income, your savings, and your debt. You might just leave the interest rate at the default setting—the day's current 30-year rate with one point added in—because you're just starting to shop around for mortgages and you might not know what kinds of rates lenders are willing to give you.

Once you've entered this information, you get a very general overview of how much a typical lender might give you. If you earn $78,000 a year and have $8,000 squirreled away while paying $300 to debtors each month, Homefair's calculator says you can buy a home worth $135,363, with a mortgage of $131,302. That's after you apply all your savings to a modest down payment and the closing costs. (By the way, don't worry that the calculator has factored in a down payment of just 3%.)

With all the stiff competition among lenders to shell out mortgages, very few people can't get a loan just because they haven't got 20% of the home's value saved up. In fact, many perfectly reputable lenders will give you a mortgage with 5% or less up front. The catch? You'll have to pay something called private mortgage insurance, or PMI, for a number of years, and you might not get as low an interest rate as you would otherwise.) As you can see, the calculator has figured a monthly private mortgage insurance payment of $109.

Be Wary:
Sometimes, in order to use a calculator at a vendor's site, you may wind up giving out certain information, such as your email address, that could set you up for some serious junk mail from that company down the line. And of course, you'll be fed a line about how good the mortgages are at that particular company.

Bits and Bytes:
The days of mandatory 20% down payments are gone, although we believe that a minimum 20% down payment is the best way to go for most home-buyers in order to avoid the dreaded PMI.

*Homefair's calcu-
lator automati-
cally estimates
PMI if you put less
than 20% down.*

At the same time, Homefair invites you to click over to its
Preferred Lender page for some more details on certain mortgages. That's the site's profit motive kicking in—except that those
lenders pay a fee to be listed there. You can get out now, or
maybe you can check them out further if you're curious. Overall,
this is a fairly soft sell.

Now let's compare it to Countrywide's Affordability calculator at
http://www1.countrywide.com/Calculators/default.asp.

Once you type in your data, you'll get another surprise. Using the
same income, debt, and savings you plugged into Homefair's calculator (and saying you live in Ohio), you get three different
answers about how much of a loan you can afford. In this case, it
varies from $123,823 to $89,695 as your maximum mortgage
loan for a home worth no more than $131,516 to $94,416. The
range is the result of searching various loan programs at
Countrywide and giving you as many options as possible. Of
course, they offer to explain the various programs in more detail.

The lesson: Regardless of the type of mortgage calculator you
use, results can vary dramatically from site to site with the same
basic data. Don't take any one site's word too literally. These calculators are intended to give you just a rough sense of how big a
mortgage you can handle, and they don't guarantee that you'll

even get a mortgage for that amount. They're starting points, not carved-in-stone certainties. So you should try three or four different calculators to ascertain the mortgage amount that's right for you.

For more information on determining how much you can spend on a home, see *Sams Teach Yourself e-Real Estate Today* by Jack Segner.

Getting the Mortgage You Want

Now that you know generally how much you can afford to spend on a new house, you need a mortgage. "But wait," you say, "I haven't found a house yet! What am I doing getting a mortgage?" Think again. It helps to be pre-approved or pre-qualified for a mortgage before you even go house-shopping because it shows potential sellers that you're motivated. In many parts of the country, the housing market is so competitive that you can lose out on your dream house if you wind up in a multiple bidder situation where two or more buyers want the same house. The sellers and their agent get to choose who to sit down and deal with. Generally, anyone with a mortgage in hand, or at least a promise of a mortgage, can move to the front of the line.

Visiting the mortgage shopping sites is helpful at the beginning of your mortgage application process, when you need to compare interest rates and points. *Points*, in case you don't already know, represent the cost of getting a particular mortgage. Each point is one percentage point of the loan amount—for instance, two points on a $200,000 mortgage is $4,000, an amount that would be charged to you. Naturally, it's best to find a mortgage with no points—and they're out there. That's where these mortgage shopping sites can really come in handy.

Remember how we said you never really need to meet your mortgage bankers? It's true. Most big mortgage lenders, as well as particular mortgage loan originators—the guys who work for the lenders and who actually pocket the commission from each loan they sell—are only too happy to do business with you over the phone or Internet. So are mortgage brokers, the army of people who can track down a loan for you, at the rate you want, in return for compensation from either you or the bank you eventually get the loan with. When using the Internet to get a loan, you'll still need to supply the reams of personal and financial information that you'd bring to an office, but you can do it by email or good

Bits and Bytes:
Fortunately, there are mortgage-related Web sites that are characterized not by the hard sell but by friendly, unbiased information designed to help make mortgage shopping easier. These sites, some of which are run by the federal government, can educate you on the finer points of all mortgages, including the ones offered under government guidelines, such as those backed by the Federal Housing Administration.

old U.S. mail. And you can bite your nails and pull your hair out at home instead of in front of some impassive banker. But a word of warning: most of these sites will definitely carry a strong hard-sell flavor.

Let's continue mortgage shopping by visiting one of these kinder, gentler educational sites. Mortgage.Interest.com is an online off-shoot of Mortgage Market Information Services Mortgage Guide, which publishes a mortgage newsletter. It's a good general site, with a message board and plenty of useful, unbiased background information. For example, go to the site's Consumer's Guide to Mortgage Lock-ins, which explains how to lock in—or guarantee—a particular interest rate on a mortgage before actually buying a house:

Try It Yourself ▼

1. Pull up the home page at *http://www.interest.com*.

2. Click the first item on the list of topics: 1st Time Home Buyers Start Here.

3. Great! You're on your own page, just for first-timers. You've got a nice selection of information, ranging from the Mortgage Topic of the Week to the Bad Credit OK Center. Scroll down until you see the Interest.com Bookshelf. Click on it.

4. See a bunch of books? It's almost as good as—or better than—the library! Select the first book on the left, the one on lock-ins. It takes you straight to the first page. Ten more pages follow; just read them at your own rate.

▲

So, with just three clicks from the home page, you're getting an education on the finer points of mortgage lock-ins. Not too shabby, eh? While you're here, you might want to bookmark this site because it's very comprehensive. In addition to news of the mortgage world, it also happens to have many of the other features we've already discussed, such as a mortgage calculator to figure out how much of a mortgage you can afford.

Now let's try some mortgage comparison shopping. We'll start by going to two quite different sites.

Bankrate.com

Bankrate.com has a few good things going for it in the mortgage area. As its name suggests, it specializes in offering objective, detailed information on interest rates (not just for mortgages, but also for other types of bank loans, credit cards, and auto financing). You might want to make this information a starting point in any mortgage search. Don't think that interest rates won't make much difference. One extra percentage point on a 30-year, $150,000 mortgage adds up to tens of thousands of dollars over the lifespan of the loan. Bankrate is set up both as an independent information site on interest rates and a tool to search for specific lenders.

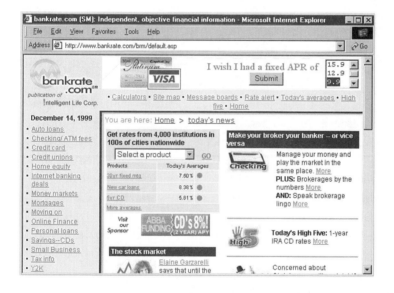

Bankrate.com offers unbiased information on all kinds of interest rates.

Look at the home page. Every day the site posts the current average 30-year fixed mortgage rate, with an arrow indicating whether rates are rising or falling. That's useful right off the bat. If you see a lot of arrows pointing up day after day, you might want to get moving before you're priced out of the market—that's right, rates are on the rise. Right above it, you're invited to select a product and get an interest rate quote. If you choose mortgages, you can then select your state, city, and the type of mortgage you're considering—a 30-year fixed-rate, for example, or a one-year adjustable rate. There's even an option for problem credit. (Such mortgages, called *nonconforming* in lender jargon, come with significantly higher rates from the start, but if your credit isn't AAA, they can be your best bet for owning a home). Once you've plugged in your data, you're rewarded with a detailed chart showing lenders, their latest interest rates (based on a $125,000 mortgage), and contact information, including links to their own sites. An important note: These lenders aren't paying to be listed here. This is truly objective information, dug up by a team of researchers in Bankrate's offices who pretend to be consumers calling innocently about the day's mortgage rate. Low or high, the rates are then posted here.

LoanWeb

The LoanWeb mortgage shopping site (*http://www.loanweb.com*) goes a step further in that it actually initiates contact with potential lenders on your behalf. You start by typing in some basic data over on the right: ZIP code, home phone area code, state, and the type of loan you're in the market for. From there, LoanWeb tells you your state's average interest rate and asks for more detailed information, such as what you'd actually provide on a mortgage application—debt, income, credit history, how much cash you'll put down, whether or not you've already found a house, and so on. This information is then forwarded to lenders, who contact you in a few days with an evaluation, potential rates, and so on. Essentially, it's a way for you to fill out an application that could go to any of hundreds of lenders, rather than going from bank to bank repeating the same process over and over again.

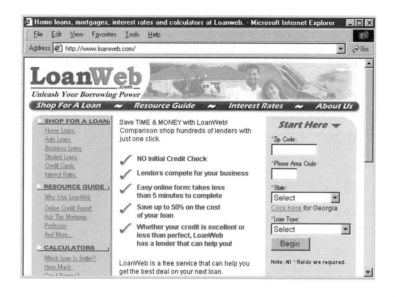

Information you provide on LoanWeb is sent to potential lenders.

LoanWeb is a pretty bare-bones site. Other than some calculators, links to lists of real estate agents, and the like, there are no frills here—no articles, no news, not a lot of original content, just an interface with a network of lenders. But if you're comfortable with mortgage basics, you don't feel like wading through lots of other information and articles, and you don't mind giving out personal financial information online (the site says it's completely secure and makes a point not to ask for personal data such as Social Security numbers), it's a good way to initiate contact with lenders. Just prepare for a deluge of junk mail from the mortgage banks to which it's shipping your data.

Now let's look at Web sites set up by specific lenders and brokers that allow you to go the whole nine yards and apply online. Many lender sites, like Countrywide, serve a few purposes. They present a full complement of mortgage-related information—the day's interest rates, calculators, and so on—and they can be pretty useful as long as you know you're dealing with people who want to sell you something. And for people who aren't into doing mortgage business over the Internet, these sites act as an introduction to the banks, posting toll-free telephone numbers to call or addresses of nearby branches.

Bits and Bytes:

Remember how we said you can get a mortgage without even setting foot in a lender's office? You've already started that process by shopping around the different online lenders for rates you like.

Other sites are run by brokers, who are also looking for your business and would dearly like to hook you up with a mortgage lender (remember, they get a cut of the deal). They'll take your application and farm it out, much as you'd do yourself with some of those mortgage shopping sites.

Then there are online mortgage bankers, who do almost the whole process over the Internet. This is a new breed of mortgage bank that has appeared in the past several years as the Internet has matured.

One of them is *http://mortgagebot.com/*. Let's explore this site a bit and see what you need to do to make a deal online. First, look at the home page. You're encouraged to apply online and be pre-approved in 15 minutes. Wow. Remember when we told you it's a good idea to become pre-approved before you look at homes because you come across as a more serious, capable home buyer? It may seem weird to get pre-approved for a mortgage in less time than you can buy and eat a Big Mac, but don't worry about it. Don't worry about how a seller might view your pre-approval, either. This lender is part of a reputable bank called Marshall & Isley Corp, familiar to Minnesotans as M&I Bank. There's nothing to be afraid of here. Speed and silly names are just part of the Internet. And, you'll notice, Mortgagebot is limiting its applicants to those with traditional 20% down payments, so it isn't exactly handing out loans left and right.

Mortgagebot can get you pre-approved in 15 minutes as long as you've got 20% to put down.

Take it for a spin and pretend you're applying (don't worry—you can stop at any point with no obligation).

▼ **Try It Yourself**

1. First, click Apply Now. At the bottom-right corner of the page, you're asked to fill in your name and click the green arrow.

2. Now you're on a first-name basis. Fill in your email address and create a password. Click the green arrow again.

3. Here's your introduction to the basic Mortgagebot process. The emphasis all along is on ease and speed. Notice how, even though you haven't filled out a single form, the friendly little animated red dot (his name is Botman) says, "Your application is 12% complete!"

4. On the next page, answer the question about whether you're buying or refinancing your home. Click the option that says you're buying and haven't signed an agreement with the seller. Click that green arrow again.

5. A-ha! The application. Go ahead, fill it out. It's at least four pages, so just proceed through it page by page. Click on the green arrow.

6. You're now looking at a chart of various mortgage options, based on the information you entered on your application: a 30-year loan, 15-year loan, fixed-rate or adjustable, with different interest rates, points, and monthly payments. Below that are estimates of closing costs to go with each loan. And at the very bottom, you're asked to select one of these loan options. Do so and go on to the next page.

7. Now Mortgagebot has summarized the loan for which you're applying and asks you to print it out for your records. Move to the next page.

8. The application continues with questions about your income, assets, and debt. (Hey, no one ever said applying for a mortgage was easy, even online!) Keep filling it out, even though it stretches across several Web pages. During the process, the site will ask your permission to order a credit report. The whole time, Botman will tell you how far along you are—75%, 82%, and so on.

9. Finally, you've reached the end of the application. Click on the big green bar labeled Submit for Instant Approval. Almost immediately you'll find out if you've been pre-approved or denied. Remember, this is just a pre-approval. If you can't verify some of the information you provided on the application, the mortgage won't stick. The remaining few steps simply ask you to order a kit with the actual documents needed to process a mortgage. If you're just trying it out for fun, this is where you want to stop before you have to ante up an origination fee. Otherwise, keep going.

Applying for a mortgage online isn't for everyone, but now you see how easy it can be to at least get pre-approved online. And once you've found a mortgage deal you can live with and a lender you like, you're ready to find your dream house.

Buying and Selling Your Home

Bits and Bytes:

The Internet is a huge timesaver when you're just starting to look at homes, and it's fun, too. You can peek at house after house from the comfort of your own home. If you really like a house, you can always make an appointment to go see it in person.

Whether you're buying or selling your home, the Internet lends itself naturally to either activity. Prospective buyers can browse properties, from across the country or around the corner, without ever setting foot in the actual neighborhood.

Let's start by looking at some of the big national sites, which might have hundreds or thousands of real estate listings in towns and cities across the country. Basically, you can search for homes in your area or any area you'd like to move to. In some cases, these Web sites might be the same ones you used at the beginning of the process if you were relocating. These big sites have some advantages and disadvantages.

First, the advantages. Sites like HomeWeb, Homefair.com, Realtor.com, and NewHomeNetwork, which are all nationwide, have size on their side. Because of their size, they can be more comprehensive, offering links to dozens of real estate agents, mortgage providers, moving companies, and others you need to buy or sell a home. In fact, many of these sites have functions similar to the sites we've already discussed in this chapter. Some might also have useful background information on financing a home, closing on a sale, and so on. And all of them have search functions, which is how you find and view the homes for sale. You simply type in your parameters—state, city, the size of the home you want, and your price range. If you're relocating far away, this ability to search state-by-state and city-by-city can be invaluable.

Now, the disadvantages. Because these Web sites are national, their listings of homes in some areas of the country can be spotty. You might find that there's not a single listing for your town, but that certainly doesn't mean there are no homes for sale with your criteria in that area. It just means that the site isn't catching all the available listings, probably because it doesn't have any relationships set up with real estate agencies in that area. It's very frustrating to type in your town and have the system report back that no listings match your criteria, when you weren't exactly looking for a mansion—just a three-bedroom with 1 and a half bathrooms for around $200,000. You know listings like that are out there, but they're not showing up on this site. This happens regularly on these kinds of sites.

Let's look at a house on one of these sites so you can see their advantages and disadvantages for yourself. Try Realtor.com at *http://www.realtor.com*, which claims to offer more than 1.3 million homes on its site—let's hope some of them are where you want them to be. Say you're looking for a house in Northbrook, Illinois, a suburb of Chicago. Select your state—Illinois—and click Go. You get a nice map of the state, with various towns and counties marked. Click on Cook County on the map. Now you get a smaller, more detailed map of Chicago's North Shore. It's a little frustrating that the site didn't just take you straight to Cook County; it's still showing you other counties nearby. But you're getting warmer (funny, and you thought you were moving to Chicago!). Click on Cook County Northeast in the list of areas, and note that you also have to know which part of the county Northbrook is in. If you're unfamiliar with the area, this can be pretty frustrating.

Okay, now you have another map, this one showing Northbrook and its adjacent towns. You also have a scrollbar on the left, so move down, select Northbrook, and then click Continue. Select your home type (single family, etc.) and click Continue again. Now the site tells you how many listings it has in this area. But it hasn't screened them for size or price yet, so you need to plug in more information before you start packing. Do that next. Let's say $250,000 for your starting price, with three bedrooms and at least one bath. You can choose how many listings you'd like to view at once, starting with three at a time.

Click the Search button. Bingo! You've hit pay dirt. There's a picture of the first house right there on your screen, complete with price and description. Underneath is its listing agent's phone number and address—maybe even his or her picture. This site also has a nifty option to give you detailed data on the house's surroundings, which you access by clicking on the box below Neighborhood Info. You get a still more detailed map showing the surrounding neighborhood, how many schools there are, neighborhood density, whether or not it's a kid-oriented area, and average home price and age.

A megasite such as Realtor.com lets you preview homes from the comfort of your own.

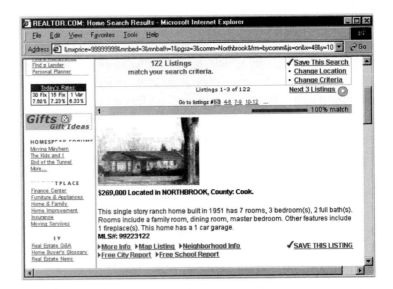

As you can see, there are a number of pros and cons to using this service. Because it's national, it took quite a few steps to home in on the town you were looking at, and it would have been even harder had you not known a few things about your town, such as what part of the county it's in. But once you got there, you did find listings with your criteria and you were able to check out very specific details about different neighborhoods—something a less comprehensive site probably wouldn't offer.

But suppose you're not interested in looking at pictures of houses. You want to see the real thing. For that, it helps if you find a real estate agent. There are sites for this, too. Try going to Agentscout.com, *http://www.agentscout.com*, a listing of agents across the country. The site says it screens agents by how long they've been in the business (the minimum is five years) and how well they perform (those that don't are kicked out). In exchange for being listed here, the agents give the site a piece of their sales commissions.

The first thing you get on the site is another search engine. Type in your state. You get a list of towns. Unfortunately, it's hardly every city or town in the state. AgentScout is limited by how many real estate agents it can sign up who are willing to share their commissions with the site—and if nobody in Mayberry wants to play ball, well, AgentScout can't give you much of anything in Mayberry. But if you do find your town on the list, click on it. You'll get a form where you enter the usual basic information: your price range, the size of the house you want, and so on. You can also say when you'd like an agent to contact you and where—office, home, evenings, mornings. And you can say whether you're interested in buying or selling a home. When you're finished, you send in your form and an agent is referred to you.

Finally, what if you're interested in selling your home on your own? (A strategy we don't recommend for most sellers!) That makes you a proponent of FSBO, or For Sale By Owner. You have plenty of company because more and more people are trying their luck marketing their own home to buyers rather than paying a commission to an agent.

There are a few sites just for FSBOs, which will teach you how to sell your home and give you a place to show it off to potential buyers. One of the more extensive sites is named, fittingly enough, FSBO.com. At this site, you can obtain products such as a sign to put in your front yard, as well as manuals and guides to selling a home yourself. And if you're considering buying an

FSBO, FSBO.com also maintains listings of houses for sale by owner, which you can search in much the same manner as the other home-finding sites. The catch? Its search function is far less sophisticated. You can only search an entire state at a time, which means you'll be scrolling past an awful lot of houses just to see if there's one in your area.

Closing the Deal

So you have your mortgage in hand and you've found your dream house. Now you need to huddle with the folks who'll help you close the deal: home inspectors and attorneys, in addition to the real estate agents and mortgage bankers with whom you've worked all along.

Bits and Bytes:

Attorneys will walk you through the contract with the buyer or seller, oversee the title search (in which the owners prove that they really own the house they're selling), and hold your hand through the closing process of signing a bunch of forms and writing a bunch of checks.

Home inspectors, as you probably know, are an integral part of buying and selling any property. If you're buying, you want someone to "kick the tires" and tell you exactly what you're getting into—that the roof will need replacing in five years, for instance, or that there's a water seepage problem in the basement. Unfortunately, you can't always count on a home seller to tell you these things, even though they're supposed to. If you're selling, you want to know what things you might need to fix, such as the termites gnawing away at your foundation, before you put your house on the market. Knowing everything about what you're selling helps you fulfill your obligation to disclose any flaws or major problems with the house. If you don't make full disclosure, you're in for a heap of trouble.

You can find home inspectors and real estate attorneys all over the Web. Like many service professionals, many of them have developed their own sites to promote their services. Finding them is simply a matter of typing in "home inspection services" in a search engine such as Yahoo!, Excite, or Ask Jeeves. But where can you find unbiased, nonpromotional information about these services on the Internet?

Try giving Freddie Mac's site a shot. Freddie Mac actually stands for the Federal Home Loan Mortgage Corporation, a publicly chartered agency that buys and sells mortgages from lenders. By guaranteeing certain mortgages, it helps millions of everyday people qualify for mortgages and buy homes. In doing so, Freddie

Mac has taken on sort of an advocacy role for homebuyers. That's why its Web site is filled with useful home-buying information.

▼ **Try It Yourself**

1. Start by pulling up Freddie Mac's home page at *http://www.freddiemac.com*. Over on the left is a blue bar with a number of items in it. Scroll down until you see Homebuyers. Click on it.

2. Now you have a page full of home-buying resources. The second blue bullet on the page is labeled A Consumer Home Inspection Kit. Click this bullet.

3. Okay, you're in. Note that this kit tells you how to do your own inspection of a home, from top to bottom. It even includes a "schedule of normal life," or a sense of how long parts of the house are supposed to last, for everything from galvanized gutters to slate roofs (and practically every other kind of roof). And there's a handy glossary of terms. The guide is neither too brief nor too exhaustive. It's a very useful tool, but it doesn't replace an onsite inspection by a professional.

Unfortunately, this guide doesn't tell you how to hook up with a professional home inspector, and most of us wouldn't trust our own inspection even if we did use a guide such as this. If you hop back to the second page you visited, the one with all the home-buying resources on it, you won't see anything about finding or using a real estate attorney. So what can you do? Exit Freddie Mac's site, and let's check out a couple of other resources.

Many groups of professionals band together into associations, and home inspectors are no exception. As with most trade associations, they have a Web site: the American Society of Home Inspectors site at *http://www.ashi.com*. This is a good place to learn more about home inspection and perhaps even find an inspector in your area. The site has a feature called Find an Inspector, in which you enter your ZIP code to get a list of ASHI members in your area, along with their addresses, phone numbers, and Web links, as well as how far they are from the ZIP code you entered. If you're interested, you can click over to their sites.

So what about an attorney? Well, attorneys have banded together on the Internet as well. Although the official trade association for lawyers—the American Bar Association—doesn't provide an online list of its members, lawyers are a resourceful bunch. For instance, there's Legal.Net at *http://db.legal.net/ldn/welcome/ query.cfm*, at which you can search for a real estate lawyer. You'll find hundreds of them listed, even some in foreign countries— although you can't specify your geographic area if you've already specified the type of attorney you want. Still, it's a matter of scrolling down the list until you see one in your area. You should also ask your local banks which real estate attorneys they use in your area.

On Your Way

As you've seen, properly buying and selling a home is a pretty important process. You've just touched the tip of a very big iceberg here. But you've also learned that the Internet is particularly helpful in this area:

- Honing your geographic searches to communities where you might relocate is pretty easy when you use the state, city or town, ZIP code, and area code as search tools.

- Entering a few pieces of basic financial data can give you a general sense of how big a mortgage you might qualify for, and it's possible to be pre-approved for a mortgage over the Internet within a few minutes.

- It's also possible to do most of your mortgage comparison shopping over the Internet, comparing them on the basis of interest rates, closing costs, and other factors.

- Viewing prospective homes on the Internet can take a lot of the legwork out of choosing a new home.

- To find people to help you close the deal, such as attorneys and home inspectors, visit the Web sites of professional networks and trade associations.

CHAPTER 11

College—Covering the Skyrocketing Costs of Higher Education

College has never been exactly cheap, but in the past decade or so the cost of higher education has risen faster than computers become obsolete—and that's fast. Historically, the cost of college has outpaced inflation, which makes it extremely difficult for parents and students alike to keep pace with tuition, room and board, and all the ancillary costs related to life after high school. Yet, at the same time, a college degree has become more necessary to achieve the kind of success you want for your kids.

That's why it makes sense to look at college costs long before your kids are even close to going off to State U. Ideally, you should start when they're still finger painting, or possibly even younger. The longer you save and prudently invest your money, the more it can grow, so you'll have more set aside by the time your oldest child enters college. Many financial planners recommend a fairly aggressive approach to this investing plan, using individual stocks and stock mutual funds to ensure that your assets have the best shot at growing before they're needed for tuition and other college-related expenses.

The Internet is full of incredibly helpful college-related information—maybe because so many of tomorrow's college students are already prime Web surfers by the time they're 12 years old. But much of the data available on college is actually for you, their parents, so that you can make some decisions about paying for

What You'll Learn in This Chapter:

- ► How to find general information about college costs and savings.
- ► How to research financial aid and apply for it online.
- ► How to conduct scholarship searches via the Internet.
- ► How to find student loans online.

school down the line. You'll find calculators (which probably doesn't surprise you), as well as financial aid tips and assistance, scholarships, and even loans over the Internet. So let's hit the books, so to speak, and do some cramming!

Let's Get Smart

Before your son or daughter gets much older, you need to sit down and start thinking about how you'll finance the cost of higher education. Will you save for it all out of your household income? Look for scholarships or loans? Ask your child to contribute a set amount from a summer job or work-study job during the school year? There are a lot of options. But before you can even start homing in on one or two of them, you need to get a general sense of how much money you're going to need. You need to estimate your kid's future college costs.

Let's start by visiting a site run by *U.S. News & World Report*, a magazine that publishes a widely read annual college guide. You may not know that the magazine runs a Web site too: *http://www.usnews.com*. It's chock full of education-related resources designed to get you started on college planning. In addition to subjective pieces that illustrate and rank the best values among different colleges and universities, the site also contains calculators and interactive worksheets that can help you estimate your costs. Let's try one out.

Try It Yourself ▼

1. Go to the home page. Right in the center of the page is a section titled .edu, in green. You'll see several subheadings just below it in yellow—College, Graduate school, Financial Aid, and so on. Click on Financial Aid.

2. You have quite a few options on this page. Bypass most of them for now (you can always go back and explore more in a moment) and just go over to the left-hand navigation bar, in black. Under the heading Try These Tools, click the Predict College Costs? link.

3. Okay, now you're getting down to business. You're going to enter some basic information about your son or daughter's college plans on this page. Note that the site has already filled in the estimated tuition inflation rate, 6%. Unless you know something that most college planners don't, just leave it at that. Enter the number of years until your child enrolls in college—it might be 15 years for a little kid, or just a few years for a teenager. And although it could be many years until your child has any dream schools picked out, enter a few schools . If you're really not sure, just enter your own alma mater or a local college. You might try looking at three schools with different costs: one that's expensive, one you think is in the middle price range, and one that's relatively cheap, like a state college or university. Or why not have fun while you're at it—type in Harvard or Yale. (Hey, you never know how things might turn out for Junior!) Then click on Get College Information.

   If the college name you entered is ambiguous or has multiple campuses, a screen appears where you can pick the one you want.

4. On the next screen, all you need to do is click on the gray button at the bottom that reads Fill in Form.

5. You now have a nice green-and-white chart of your estimated total cost of attendance, taking into account inflation and the number of years before your son or daughter enrolls at Harvard—or wherever. In addition to breaking out tuition, room and board, personal expenses, and other costs, the site includes the difference between total costs now and total costs when your child will enroll (scary, isn't it?). And it also tosses in the four-year cost of attendance at that point (*really* scary).

You can compare the costs of attending any colleges, even your alma mater.

http://www.usnews.com/utils/dscosts - Microsoft Internet Explorer

File   Edit   View   Favorites   Tools   Help

Address http://www.usnews.com/utils/dscosts   Go

Total cost of attendance

School (State)	Boston College	Webster University	
Tuition and fees	$22,256	$12,250	
Room and board	$8,250	$5,440	
Books and supplies	$600	$1,600	
Transportation	N/A	N/A	
Personal expenses	$1,000	N/A	
Total cost of attendance for 1998-99 academic year:	$32,106	$19,290	
First year cost of attendance in years at 6% inflation:	$32,106	$19,290	
Four year cost of attendance in years at 6% inflation:	$140,451	$84,386	

N/A indicates that the school did not provide data to U.S. News in a certain area, or that the data is not applicable to a particular school, such as in-state or out-of-state tuition for private schools.

1. Tuition and fees for the 1998-99 academic year

You've eliminated some of the mystery from the college planning process in one pretty easy series of steps. Even if you entered completely hypothetical college choices, you have a sense of what might happen between now and when your child is ready for the old ivory tower.

But you're not done yet. Although you might have a sense of the total nut you need to crack to fund a college degree, you haven't factored in other things that can affect how much money you'll need to set aside for college. For example, how much can you and your spouse contribute, or how much can your own kid contribute? At this point, you might try a site dedicated to helping parents and students plan college costs. Where better to go than the site run by the Student Loan Marketing Association, better known as Sallie Mae, the government's agency for student loans? Go to *http://www.salliemae.com* and we'll walk through some of the resources there.

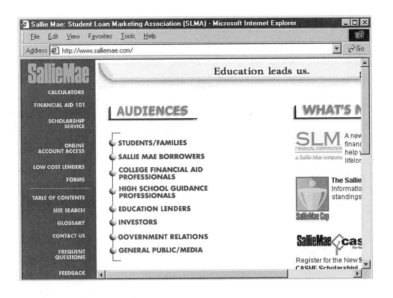

Sallie Mae offers information on more than merely student loans.

You can find a host of college calculators here that address the preceding questions and a whole lot more. Sallie Mae kindly gives you the option of downloading its CollegeCalc software (available at the Calculators link) and running the numbers on your own, or you can fill in its seven different college cost calculators while you're online. Its calculators build on each other—as you enter data into the first one, the results will automatically go into the next one as long as you hit the Next button when asked.

Although other sites (such as personal finance portals) can offer quite a bit of college financial advice, Sallie Mae's site features things such as a glossary of terms, links to college lenders, an exhaustive overview of financial aid, a scholarship search service, and even financial aid forms that you can download (more on financial aid later in this chapter).

Now you have a better idea of how much money you'll probably need. You're probably starting to panic a bit—how on earth will you amass that kind of money? Before the nail-biting turns into hair-pulling, spend some time with sites that help you develop a strategy to start saving and investing to cover college costs.

Not surprisingly, the personal finance portals all have sections that deal with college planning. One particularly in-depth site that's full of college savings ideas and strategies is MSN MoneyCentral's site at *http://www.moneycentral.com*.

Try It Yourself ▼

1. Open your browser to the home page.

2. In orange type, you see the heading Family & College. Follow that link to an entire section on this topic.

3. From there, you'll see some links under the heading Quick Reference. One of them is labeled College Planning. Click on that and it will take you to a mini-search engine of sorts.

4. Select the aspect of college planning that most appeals to you—in this case, probably Saving for College. You get a list of questions and answers about college savings strategies, covering things such as using a home equity loan to pay for tuition, the pros and cons of prepaying tuition now, whether or not custodial accounts can help you save for this purpose, whether you should save the money in your child's name or yours, and so on. Don't fret if you feel as if you're suffering information overload by the time you hit these pages. Just be glad there's so much there!

These straightforward, no-nonsense questions and answers will prepare you to start setting aside some money for college.

The State You're In

As you develop a strategy for saving college money, you might consider an option called state-run or state-sponsored savings plans. These are relatively new plans that are offered by many state governments to give parents certain tax breaks—and they don't necessarily require that you live in the state that's running the plan that you choose. Each state's plan is slightly different, so how do you choose one over another?

You can review state-run college savings plans by checking out a site run by the College Savings Plan Network at *http://www.collegesavings.org*. It lets you compare plans from state to state and keep track of news affecting these plans, more of which are being introduced as time goes on.

Financial Aid

No matter how early you get a jump on college saving and investing, chances are pretty good that you'll need to consider using some form of financial aid. Don't worry about it so much when your child is still in grade school or junior high, but when your son or daughter enters high school, it's time to start mapping out a financial aid strategy.

Your first stop ought to be an authority on overall financial aid, and the Web site run by the National Association of Student Financial Aid Administrators is a good one—nicely produced, well-organized, and full of useful information. You can reach it at *http://www.nasfaa.org*. The site contains detailed overviews on the many types of loans, aid, and grants available to college students, definitions of financial aid, and worksheets that help you plan out your kid's aid package.

Bits and Bytes:
When it comes to the Internet and financial aid, you've hit pay dirt. There are many, many online resources in this area. It's one red-hot topic among parents of college-age children and the children themselves.

1. Open your browser to the home page.

2. Directly in the center of the page is a link called Financial Aid Information for Parents, Students and Counselors. Click on that link and go to the next page.

3. You have a page with a few different links. Click on the second one, titled Financial Aid: You Can Afford It. Go to the next page.

4. Now you're looking at four question marks, left to right across your screen. On the right is a short navigation bar with some handy resources—a quiz, help with financial aid applications, a calendar checklist, and a glossary. It's worthwhile to explore each of these elements because they're all useful and contain straightforward, nuts-and-bolts information. For now, let's look at one particularly useful element, which illustrates how financial aid works given one family's contribution to college costs. Click on the third question mark from the left, the one called How Is Your Financial Aid Calculated?, and go to the next page.

▼ **Try It Yourself**

5. From here, scroll down and select the link labeled A Real Life Example.

6. This is a demonstration of how one family might approach financial aid, with all the numbers neatly laid out. As you scroll down, you'll see a number of equations and calculations clearly explained. It may seem like a lot of material at first, but it's written in a very simple, straightforward manner. Go ahead—read it! You'll learn quite a bit.

The NASFAA's site is straightforward and will help you estimate a financial aid package.

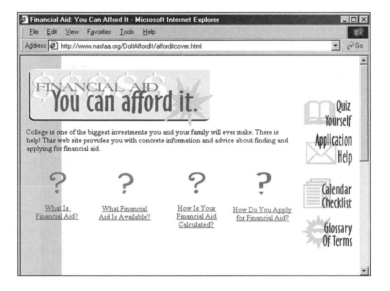

Another site with a wealth of information on financial aid is *http://www.finaid.com*, which bills itself as the Smart Student Guide to Financial Aid. It's nicely organized, with separate areas for students, parents, and counselors, and includes a section on military aid, such as the Reserve Officers Training Corps or ROTC, which may help pay for college as well. (Many other financial aid sites don't mention ROTC, despite the fact that it's long been a way to pay for college.) Overall, FinAid is useful as a sort of mini-portal for financial aid data because it allows you to perform many of the tasks you'll need to contend with when planning for and applying for financial aid, such as downloading the right application forms. Its forms section alone makes the site worth bookmarking. It exhaustively walks you through the various form deadlines, provides caveats, and offers links to toll-free helplines and so forth.

When it's time to apply for federal student aid via the government's Federal Student Financial Assistance program, you can do so online by using the program's main site at *http://www.fafsa. ed.gov*. (Warning: you might want to dim your monitor. For some odd reason, this site's home page uses one of the brightest shades of neon green we've *ever* seen.) It's a no-frills site, but it takes a little of the legwork out of the arduous process of filing financial aid forms. Here, students fill out a Free Application for Federal Student Aid (FAFSA) form. Everyone, whether they think they'll be eligible for financial aid or not, can fill out this form—and in fact, your kids should do it themselves.

Scholarships

Scholarships can be a very important part of the financial aid process. In fact, many of the sites you've already visited in this chapter include scholarship resources. As college costs have risen over the past several years, more and more students from all walks of life have been forced to consider scholarships... beefing up the competition for the limited pool of funds. Are you out of luck? Not quite. Finding a list of available scholarships has never been easier, thanks to the Internet's ability to conduct detailed information searches. You might be pleased to know that the advent of the Internet has spawned an entire cottage industry for scholarship search engines.

Before we get started, however, a word of warning: Along with the boom in scholarship search engines comes a profit motive for many of the engines' creators. Some of the scholarship sites you'll encounter aim to sell you expensive books, computer printouts, and other services related to finding scholarship money. Don't pay for something you can get for free. Some scholarship searchers will charge $50 or so to supply you with a list of scholarships, when you can usually do this for free.

Bits and Bytes:

When it comes to online scholarship offers, look for strings attached if you suspect something's too good to be true.

Moreover, you'll encounter a few scholarship scams online. Scams such as these have always been out there, but the Internet has allowed them to prosper in recent years. Be wary of any supposed scholarship offers that use words like "guaranteed," "fee-based," or similarly suspicious-sounding terms. No scholarship is guaranteed.

That said, there are a number of truly useful scholarship search engines. One of the best is the College Board's site at *http://www.collegeboard.org*, despite the fact that the College Board is technically a sort of vendor that's eager to impress you. It's best known as the creator of the SAT (Scholastic Aptitude Test), that bane of high school students everywhere. But its Web site is especially helpful, particularly when it comes to scholarship searches and other basic college-planning resources. The College Board site has morphed from a mere purveyor of some mighty intimidating tests to an all-around online college planner. Let's give it a whirl.

Try It Yourself ▼

1. Go to the home page. Over on the left you'll see several bulleted links. Click on the first one, Students and Parents.

2. On this page, scroll down a bit until you see a red bullet point next to a section labeled Searches. You have a choice of colleges, scholarships, careers, and something mysterious called SAT codes. Select the link labeled Scholarships and click to the next page.

3. Welcome to the Scholarship Search. Read the bit of background presented and click on the green button marked Continue at the bottom.

4. The search is starting. You'll read a few instructions and then move down to fill in the information—starting with your year in school, any other financial aid you're going to have, and any specific type of scholarship, such as one for music performance. Beyond that, you must enter basic biographical and demographic information related to the different scholarships available, such as those offered by particular employers, veterans' groups, or benevolent organizations. When

you're finished, click the gray button at the end labeled Submit Form.

5. A-ha! Now you should be looking at a list of links to programs that may be able to offer you a scholarship. Clicking on any of them will send you right to that program's Web site, and you can take it from there. Not bad, huh? Now if only *getting* the actual scholarship were this easy....

Let's compare this scholarship search engine to another one that's more community-oriented than anything else. This time visit Fresch at *http://www.fresch.org*. This site has a much different goal than the College Board's, which is polished and rather corporate in appearance. Fresch, which is aimed more at your college-bound kid than you, is funky and, well, fresh. But don't be fooled by its tie-dyed logo. Fresch contains helpful resources in the scholarship area, including an overview of some of those scams mentioned earlier in this section, discussion forums about scholarships and financial aid issues, and a massive database of roughly 1,900 scholarship providers. With Fresch's fun, snappy approach to scholarships, you might even consider "assigning" your kids to explore the site themselves and report back to you with their findings; they may appreciate some of the site's quirkier aspects more than you do. Either way, it's a site worth checking out.

Fresch seems geared more toward your child than you, but don't let its hip appearance dissuade you from browsing its resources.

Staying In Budget

Once your kid makes it to college, how is she going to keep her expenses in line? College is no time to let expenses get out of whack—and yet for many college kids, managing money while on their own for the first time can be overwhelming. Remember Family Money's Web site from Chapter 10? You might want to check out its handy semester budget worksheet, which helps college kids sort out their own finances from one school term to the next. Go to *http://www.familymoney.com*, choose Kids & Money on the left menu, and then choose Semester Budget Worksheet near the end of the page. Here, kids can enter any income they receive from jobs held during school, as well as from student loans and even from you—that is, financial assistance you send them from home during the school year. They can then reconcile that income against their expenses, such as laundry, club dues, and so on. The worksheet is presented in a clean, no-nonsense format that won't intimidate even the greenest of freshmen.

College Loans

So you've scrimped and saved for your kids' college expenses, brown-bagging your lunch and staying with in-laws for vacations. You've filled out reams of financial aid forms, You and your child have both worn your fingers to nubs searching for scholarships online. Yet you still face a shortfall when it comes to those pesky college bills. What's next?

No question: a student loan. Don't fret about it. Student loans have been around practically as long as colleges have. Okay, maybe not quite *that* long, but long enough that you probably had one yourself. You're hardly alone in taking this next step in financing college. The world of student loans is a big and varied one, cluttered with lenders offering various student loan products... some good, some bad.

In some cases, Sallie Mae will wind up with your child's private student loan, which it buys from the bank that originated the loan with your son or daughter. Sallie Mae then services this loan—that is, it sends your kid those little booklets of loan payment coupons when they're out of college and hopefully in a paying job. Because Sallie Mae is a quasi-governmental agency, and because the government wants college kids to get these loans, your son or daughter will get a favorable interest rate without any collateral or credit history, and won't even need you to cosign their loan. They're on their own. In other cases, your child may take out a Stafford loan, which is a government-sponsored student loan also given at a favorable interest rate.

Also, you may consider taking out a conventional loan to help pay for your child's college tuition. Private lenders offer a variety of loans for this purpose, and you can also consider a home equity loan or line of credit, which is essentially a second mortgage or lien on your home. As with any other loan, you'll need to be approved, and chances are you won't get the same break on interest rates as your kid did on his federal loan.

It's usually not the greatest strategy to take out loans for your child's education. He can qualify for a great deal of financing from the government, at better rates and on better terms, and has a much longer time span to pay back the money—basically, from the time he graduates from college. On the other hand, you're looking at retirement in not too many years, and you'll need to conserve your capital for that purpose. Most financial planners suggest that you hold off on taking out your own loans for Junior's education unless he has truly exhausted all other means of getting financial aid, student loans, and scholarships.

So where does your kid find these loans? They're not exactly hiding. The Internet is rife with offers for student loans. If you and your child have been scanning through some of the sites in this chapter, you've no doubt seen a bunch of offers for student loans, as well as the appropriate resources and information. Great— you've done some of the legwork already. But there are other sites that specialize in helping you and your kid find the right student loans. One of them is aptly named eStudentLoan, and it's found online at *http://www.estudentloan.com*. Let's visit it and see how it works.

eStudentLoan allows you to compare lenders to get the best rates.

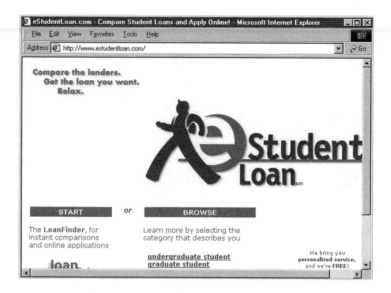

eStudentLoan starts out by asking you to select the type of student your son or daughter is—that is, an undergraduate or a grad student. Once you've done that, you're offered a look at lenders for all kinds of loans—not all of them strictly student-oriented, but some that can be applied toward college costs. For instance, the site lists links to lenders of home equity loans. The site's LoanFinder option will give you a list of lenders based on your state, intended college or university, and other factors. You can then contact lenders or arrange for them to email you. It's a useful tool that can cut much of the time involved in finding lenders.

It makes a lot of sense to revisit the Sallie Mae Web site now. You might recall that this site packs in substantial information about lenders and includes a lender search feature of its own. You just need to select the link marked Low Cost Lenders from the blue navigation bar on Sallie Mae's home page (*http://www.salliemae. com*, in case you forgot). You fill in your state and the type of student loan you want, private or Stafford, and you get a list of lenders and their phone numbers. One drawback to this search function is that the list doesn't include recent interest rates or any other relevant information on these lenders' products. You'll have to follow up with them on your own.

Finally, parents who are driven to distraction by the overwhelming process of planning and paying for their kids' college might want to check out a community site designed just for them. It's *http://www.collegeparents.org*, run by the College Parents of America. Although you do have to ante up $25 a year, you might find that talking to some like-minded parents may go a long way toward helping you sort through this frustrating yet rewarding process.

On Your Way

At this point, you may not be exactly ready to start packing Junior off to college, but we hope you're feeling a lot more confident about his chances of affording it. College doesn't have to be an insurmountable challenge—financially, at least.

- It's best to get an early start with college planning, even when your child is in grade school (or sooner!). You can use online calculators to help you predict the cost of college by the time she's ready to ship out.

- Financial aid can be a bewildering process filled with forms, deadlines, and rules, but you can get a head start on it by using Web sites devoted to financial aid assistance.

- Scholarships may not have gotten any easier to win, but they're now a lot easier to find through online scholarship search engines.

- You can shop around for different college loan providers by using sites set up specifically for that purpose.

PART V

Securing Your Golden Years

CHAPTER 12

Retirement—Planning and Financing Your Golden Years

Ah, retirement. Languid days on the beach, around-the-world cruises, surprise visits with the grandchildren… Who doesn't get a little wistful at the idea of retirement? It's our payback after years and years of getting up at 7 a.m., dealing with bosses, commuting, writing memos—you name it.

But let's face it: as much as we'd all like to see ourselves living it up during our golden years, retiring with the same lifestyle we enjoy while working is tough. Even retiring with a slightly less expensive standard of living isn't so easy, especially when you consider that many of us have changed jobs several times, sent our kids to college, maybe started a new business—all things that can affect the stability and quantity of our retirement savings. Planning your retirement involves careful thought and preparation, a little risk, and lots of patience. But if you skip it, you might find yourself with a very small financial safety net to cushion your senior years. Don't overlook retirement planning. It's a key element of the whole personal financial planning picture.

As tricky as retirement planning is, and it *is* tricky, the good news is that the Internet offers a wealth of resources, both community-oriented and otherwise. If you're approaching retirement age now, you're in good company. More than 77 million baby boomers are doing the exact same thing, which has led to the creation of hundreds of retirement-focused sites on the Internet. If you're younger and you're just starting to think about retirement, you'll also benefit from the same resources.

What You'll Learn in This Chapter:

► How to locate basic retirement information on the Internet, including tools that help you gauge how much money you'll need to retire.

► How to find your way around different retirement savings vehicles using online resources.

► What financial planners do and how to search for one who will provide assistance with retirement planning.

Getting Your Retirement Planning Up and Running

Do you know what retirement *really* means? It doesn't just mean endless days of leisure. In most cases, it means living on funds that generally come from five sources: Social Security, pension plans, tax-deferred savings plans (such as IRAs), savings, and investments. Except for Social Security, these are finite, predetermined funds that you amass during your working years. Once you retire, that's it—you can't go back and add more to your pension plan or start saving at the same rate you did when you were 45. If your retirement assets don't keep pace with inflation and your lifestyle, your only choice is to start cutting back and stretching those assets further. That's when retirement stops being so golden and starts taking on a darker hue.

With careful planning, those sources of retirement funds have many years to grow. By the time you need these assets, you could be sitting on substantial wealth, or at least enough of a cushion to be quite comfortable. All you need to do at that point is allocate your assets in a conservative manner to ensure their stability, and stay within your means. In many cases, your assets will outlive you, and your heirs will be lucky enough to inherit what remains.

For more information on inheritance, see Chapter 13, "Wills and Estate Planning—Taking Care of Your Heirs."

So how do you put yourself in that fortunate position? Start early by educating yourself on the fundamentals of retirement. It's not so much a lifestyle as a financial state of mind, one that you can adopt long before you actually stop working. Think of retirement in monetary terms, not leisure terms. Become familiar with the many aspects of retirement planning now so that you'll be prepared.

There are a number of Web sites that can help you do this. As you might expect, most personal finance portals have big sections focusing on retirement. Addressing the needs of retirees and pre-retirees is an enormous part of what they're all about in the first place—not to mention that most of them carry advertising aimed at this affluent section of the population. By now you probably know these sites well enough to visit and explore their retirement sections on your own, so let's not go there just now. Instead, let's look at some other general sites that offer good basic retirement education—enough to get your feet wet, at least.

One of these is Quicken.com, which you've checked out once or twice before this point. Quicken, run by Intuit, a vendor of software, is chock-full of resources on a variety of financial topics, and retirement is no exception. Go to *http://www.quicken.com* and click on the big yellow tab labeled Retirement at the top of your screen (or, for a shortcut that bypasses the home page, just go to *http://www.quicken.com/retirement*). This section of the site is so comprehensive, it might as well be an entirely new home page. The page is nicely organized, too, offering you a selection of tools, links, searches, and tips, as well as a section titled Retirement Basics where you should spend some time right off the bat.

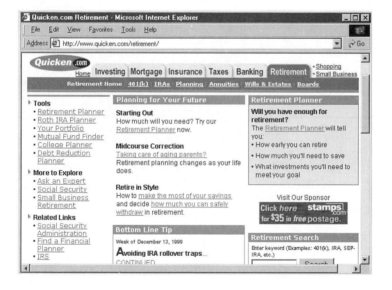

Retirement planning may be the second most popular personal finance activity on the Web after online trading.

Here you'll find solid definitions of different tax-deferred retirement savings plans, some of which you may not realize you qualify for. Did you know that if you're self-employed, you can (and should) open a Keogh plan and set aside funds for retirement, paying taxes on them later?

One particularly advantageous feature is a search function under the Related Links section on the left, which helps you find a financial planner. This kind of functionality illustrates just what a good resource this Web site can be.

Another helpful general retirement-oriented site is run by the American Savings Education Council, a nonprofit organization aimed at educating people on the need to save for the future, not just for retirement but for purposes such as college tuition. You may reach the council's Web site at *http://www.asec.org*. Here you can get started on a particularly critical piece of your basic retirement education and planning: figuring out how much money you'll need to invest and save in order to retire with a lifestyle comparable to what you have now. Let's see how it works.

The American Education Savings Council offers good advice on savings for all kinds of life events besides retirement.

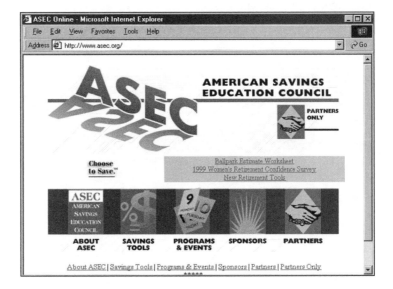

Try It Yourself ▼

1. Open your browser to the home page.

2. Along the bottom of the page are links to sections of the site. Choose the one labeled Savings Tools.

3. The very first heading, Ballpark Estimate, is what you want. Below it, written in gray, are several links offering access to an interactive version of the estimator, a non-interactive version, a Spanish version, and so on. For now, choose the first one—the interactive version.

4. Now you're in. Read the basic instructions for using the estimator, and then scroll down and start typing in the information it asks for. Note that the very first question asks for your gross annual income, followed by 70% of that income. The rule of thumb in retirement planning is that you need approximately 70% to 75% of your average yearly income for the five years prior to retirement in order to maintain a comparable lifestyle in the future. As you proceed through the questionnaire, it will fill in some numbers for you according to a formula it uses. Leave those numbers in the boxes and keep going through the questionnaire.

5. By the time you get to the bottom, you're given a number that represents how much money you'll need to save to keep your standard of living—you don't even need to wait for the response. And hopefully you're not in for too much of a shock when you get your response.

You're not done yet. In addition to some other fun stuff, including thoughtful quizzes, the American Savings Education Council site offers a useful tool called the Retirement Readiness Rating, or R^3. You can determine your R^3 by entering similar information into an interactive worksheet. To reach it, just go back to the Savings Tools page (you can click your browser's Back button to get there). Then click on What Is Your R^3? This quiz seems pretty simple at first, but give it a chance. It's a good snapshot of where you stand now, which in turn will give you an idea of the steps you need to take now to get your retirement preparations underway in earnest.

You'll also find that some non-financial Web sites still contain retirement assistance, much of it more community-oriented. For instance, you might visit Third Age, a community Web site for people over the age of 45, at *http://www.thirdage.com*. Third Age is oriented around lifestyles, and retirement is certainly part of that for people in this age group. The site offers a variety of forums on money, as well as a section on finances that's heavily skewed toward retirement issues.

Another type of Web site that can help you sort through the myriad online resources is the retirement page offered by About.com, which you can reach at *http://www.retireplan.about.com/finance/ retireplan/mbody.htm*. This site fulfills an unusual role. Rather than compile much of its own content, it acts as a kind of directory to other Web sites dealing with retirement. There's a very long list of links in dark blue over on the left side of the screen, identified as NetLinks. Each link is an aspect of retirement, some more important than others. Choose one that you feel you need to learn more about, and you're connected to dozens of sites on each topic.

One caveat, however: Many of these links will be vendor-driven, and some of them will be quite sales-oriented. Clicking on the IRA link, for example, brings up a list of sites from the likes of Met Life, Merrill Lynch, Prudential Securities, and so forth—brokerages, insurance companies, mutual fund companies, you name it. Mixed in are a few sites that offer genuine assistance with IRAs, but they're few and relatively far between. Use About.com's Retireplan page if you're eager to track down additional retirement resources, but be aware that you'll click on an awful lot of vendor sites before you find what you want.

Retirement Savings Plans Online

At first, retirement savings plans sound like so much gobbledygook: IRA, SEP, 401(k), whatever. It may as well be alphabet soup. You may already know something about these savings vehicles, especially if your employer offers a retirement plan as an employee benefit. Regardless of their funny-sounding names, it's vital for you to know what the different retirement plans are. They're specifically designed to allow you to defer taxes on income or savings so that the money can grow to its maximum potential (depending on how you allocate and invest the assets, of course). You'll pay taxes when you take the money out at or after retirement, but at that point the assets have been growing for years on a tax-deferred basis. This saves you money. It's a winning scenario, and one you'll regret not taking part in if you don't participate in a retirement savings plan of some kind.

Perhaps the most frequently used retirement plan is the IRA, or individual retirement account. IRAs come in two forms, tax-free and tax-deferred. They allow you to contribute up to $2,000 a year (or $4,000 per married couple) tax-deferred or tax-free, and the tax-deductible IRA gives you healthy tax deductions on the money you save. You can also roll over money from another retirement account, such as a 401(k), into an IRA, adding to your tax-deferred nest egg. They have a few restrictions, such as when you can take the money out without penalty (not before age 59 and six months).

IRAs are big business. Billions of dollars are parked in them, millions of people have them, and hundreds of financial services companies sell them. Indeed, the stakes are pretty high in the IRA market, especially now as the huge baby boomer population approaches retirement age. So naturally, there's a plethora of information about IRAs out there. In fact, if you search for IRAs on just about any Internet search engine, you'll come up with hundreds of Web sites offering information on the subject. Many of them are vendor-driven sites trying to get you to open an IRA; others are written by attorneys, accountants, or financial planners eager for your business. Still others offer what appears to be dubious advice. So where can you find out all you need to know about IRAs without going crazy?

Start by going back to one of those personal finance portal sites. Yes, you're probably sick of those suckers by now, but they're so darn useful. In this case, check out the Motley Fool site. Click all the way through to *http://www.fool.com/Money/AllAboutIRAs/ AllAboutIRAs.htm*. This has to be all you'd ever want to know about IRAs, in one spot. Over on the right is a gray box with red links in it—and what a list of links. There are no fewer than 14 links here, giving you the lowdown on everything from regular IRAs vs. Roth IRAs (two of the most commonly used types) to deduction limits to an IRA glossary. If you're even the slightest bit vague on your IRA ABCs, this is the place for you. Below that box is another one offering IRA calculators, which are worth checking out.

*The Motley Fool
site is irreverent,
fun, and informa-
tional.*

Calculators are a mainstay on the Internet, and when it comes to
IRAs, they're all over the place. You'll see a lot of IRA calculators on vendors' sites—companies like Vanguard, Fidelity, and
many others that are trying to sell you IRAs. There's nothing
wrong with using calculators offered by a vendor; indeed, it's
downright convenient if you're seriously researching an IRA or
some other retirement savings plan. But not all IRA calculators
are created equal. Many of them just run the basics, showing how
your money can grow if deposited in an IRA today, or how a
Roth IRA compares to a regular IRA.

Minimum withdrawals? This refers to an IRS rule requiring you
to start taking minimum distributions from your IRA (non-Roth)
six months after you turn 70 years old. How you do it depends on
how much money is in there. Let's see how it works by using
Third Age's calculator.

Try It Yourself ▼

1. Third Age has buried its IRA withdrawal calculator in a rela-
    tively remote place on its site: *http://www.thirdage.com/
    features/money/ira/withdrawal.html.*

2. Read the brief introduction. Then scroll down to the first few question blanks and type in your date of birth. Then click the Next button.

3. You're told the exact age you will be at the end of the current calendar year—as in "age 72.45". Based on that age, you're told if you must take a minimum withdrawal this year. Now you're asked if you've designated a beneficiary for your IRA—that is, someone who will receive any remaining assets left in your account if you die. After you answer, go on to the next page by clicking on the gray button at the bottom.

4. Enter your beneficiary's date of birth and whether he or she is your spouse.

5. You're now shown a divisor, which is a factor based on you and your beneficiary's life expectancy. This factor determines your schedule for minimum withdrawals from the IRA. You're also asked to enter your IRAs account balance. Do so and move on to the final page.

6. You now receive the amount of your minimum withdrawal. This is the minimum amount you must start taking out—or *distributing*, in IRA jargon—from the account at age 70 and a half.

Tax-deductible and Roth IRAs can be pretty complicated instruments, but they're just one type of retirement savings vehicle. Another common one is the 401(k), which is an employer-sponsored plan. Only your employer can give you access to a 401(k), which is offered as a benefit. (Note that if you work in the public sector, you cannot open a 401(k). Instead you'll be offered a 403(b), which is the same type of plan but is designed specifically for public employees.)

If you're offered access to a 401(k), and you've checked out the plan's investment track record, take it! This allows you to divert a portion of your salary, tax-deferred, into an investment plan, which is in turn run by an outside company hired by your employer. You can designate a portion of your salary to be dispatched into your 401(k) account. It will mean living on slightly less take-home pay, but you'll find that your money will usually grow far more quickly in the 401(k) than if you took it out and tried saving on your own, thanks to the benefit of tax deferral. Often, an employer will sweeten the deal by adding its own contribution to your 401(k) account, which is called a *match*. Some matches are 50% of the amount you contribute each pay period; others are 100%.

Still not sure? 401(k)s have been met with great acceptance and huge popularity, and there are Web sites devoted entirely to managing and understanding them. If you're on the fence about 401(k) participation, get more familiar with these investment vehicles by going to a community site called the 401Kafe at *http://www.401kafe.com*. Marked by its cute coffee cup motif, it's filled with educational tools, message boards, commentary, a 401(k) calculator to help you figure out how much you're saving, and a search engine for more 401(k) information.

The 401Kafe is a community site that offers news, educational tools, and more.

There's more. IRAs, 401(k)s, and 403(b)s are three of the most common retirement savings plans you're likely to run into, but the list goes on and on and on. If you're not careful, you might get confused by all the different options out there. One good general site that can summarize IRAs, 401(k)s, and all the other alphabet-soup plans is RetireNet at *http://www.valic.com/valic/ valweb.nsf*. RetireNet is run by a vendor named Valic. You're unlikely to encounter a Valic sales rep knocking on your door. Instead, this company pitches itself as a retirement plan administrator to companies that offer such plans to their employees. So don't worry too much about it and just enjoy RetireNet's resources.

The best feature on this site is the detailed information on all the different tax-deferred retirement plans—not just the usual suspects like IRAs, but also more exotic plans, such as the mysterious-sounding 457 DCPs.

A Little Help from the Pros

Thanks to your efforts to educate yourself on retirement basics, you're ahead of most of your peers. Depending on your own particular financial situation, it might make sense to bring in a pro for some of the "heavy lifting." You might consider hiring a financial planner or advisor. Although financial planners can help their clients with almost any aspect of personal financial management, most people hire them specifically to help with retirement preparation. Some financial planners even have sub-specialties, concentrating on certain aspects of retirement planning, such as helping their clients conduct 401(k) rollovers into IRA plans.

Financial planners may actually be trained as attorneys, accountants, or even stockbrokers or insurance salespeople. Usually, they've taken additional courses or done some extra preparation to learn the role of financial planner, and many of them are CFPs or certified financial planners. Not all financial planners are CFPs, and you don't have to use a CFP to receive excellent financial planning advice, but it's worth considering. This trade designation (contrary to popular belief, it's not a degree, such as an attorney's J.D. degree) indicates that its recipient takes financial planning seriously enough to undergo the required courses and testing, and that he or she has agreed to abide by a professional code of ethics.

In Our Experience:
We're more comfortable with financial planners who do financial planning full-time, not part-time CPAs, lawyers, etc.

Your financial planner will go over your current financial picture and talk to you about your goals, such as when you'd like to retire, where you plan to live afterwards, what types of activities you'd like to do, and so forth. He or she should also ask you about your family, such as whether it's important to you to leave money for your heirs in a trust or will (we'll cover this in more detail in Chapter 13). After this process, the financial planner will create a plan for becoming financially secure and ready to retire in the fashion you desire. It may take years for your plan to come to fruition, or, if you're close to retirement already, it may simply require some careful deployment of your current assets.

Chances are, a big part of your financial planner's plan will involve asset allocation, which will create a mix of conservative, aggressive, and moderately aggressive investments according to how much retirement money you need and how long you have to invest in them before you need the money. For example, a young person will typically have a portfolio that is mostly stocks, which are riskier than bonds but have greater capital gains potential.

Just as you did with accountants and real estate agents, you can track down financial planners in your area by searching through their professional organizations. One of the biggest of these trade groups is the International Association for Financial Planners, or IAFP. You can reach its site at *http://www.planningpaysoff.org/index.html*. At this site, you can search a database of financial advisors by entering some personal data. Once you've found a few potential planners, you can use the same site's tips on interviewing prospective planners before agreeing to hire them. Perhaps most importantly, this site explains the many different ways in which financial planners are compensated—a critical issue to understand before you start working with any financial advisor. You'll find that some planners work for a fee, others work on commission, others work on both fees and commissions, and still others charge you a percentage of the assets they manage for you. This site clearly explains the differences in compensation so you can go out and interview potential planners without getting caught off guard when it comes down to business.

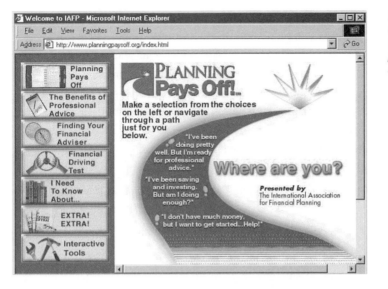

Planning Pays Off! can match you up with a financial planner in your area.

And before you start working with a financial planner, you ought to check his references—after all, this is a person who will know intimate details of your financial situation. Fortunately, you can easily check a CFP's professional status by visiting the CFP Board of Standards site at *http://www.cfp-board.org*. This is the organization that confers the CFP designation on financial advisors and then tracks their professional conduct. Why don't we see how easy it is to check up on a financial planner?

1. Go to the CFP Board of Standards site. You'll see a link on the far left of your screen marked Check the status of a CFP licensee. Click the big green button next to it labeled Go.

2. On the next page, read the explanation of the database's contents. Then type in the name of the financial planner you have in mind. You must know his first and last name and the city in which he conducts business in order to review his credentials. If you have this information handy, enter it now.

3. You receive a listing of any disciplinary records on the financial planner you're checking out.

▼ **Try It Yourself**

▲

On Your Way

Now that you know retirement isn't just about relaxing, maybe
you can feel a bit more relaxed about your planning for this phase
of life. It's important to make your financial preparations as big a
part of retirement planning as digging out the golf clubs and dust-
ing off the passport. After all, you can't retire without a stream of
income from several different sources, all of which you need to
understand and manage before your last day of work.

- For most people, retirement income is made up of five different types of income: Social Security, pension plans, tax-
  deferred retirement plans, regular savings (such as what
  you'd keep in a bank), and investments.

- You need to be able to live on about 70% to 75% of your current income during your retirement years in order to maintain
  the same standard of living you enjoy now.

- IRAs, 401(k)s, and 403(b)s are the most commonly used
  forms of retirement savings plan, and there are a number of
  resources online to help you understand their complexities.

- Financial planners, many of whom you can find online, can
  assist you in allocating your assets for sufficient retirement
  funds.

CHAPTER 13

Wills and Estate Planning—Taking Care of Your Heirs

At about the same time you really start hunkering down to do some serious retirement planning—for most of us, that's in our 40s and 50s—you'll realize that over the years you've amassed a serious asset base and you're still building. Wake-up call: In addition to your retirement planning, these assets are going to require some attention to minimize the tax bite and ensure that your loved ones receive your assets with a minimum of hassle when you're no longer around.

If you've managed your personal finances wisely, no doubt your net worth has grown while you've whittled down most of your debt. *Estate planning*—minimizing estate taxes and ensuring that as many of your assets as possible are passed on to your heirs—is the kind of problem you *want* to have. To dispel a common assumption, you don't need to be rich or even moderately well-off to need estate planning. Anyone who has accumulated assets ought to at least have a will and possibly a trust. Estate planning is not limited to millionaires.

It isn't easy to understand all facets of estate planning. It's rife with tricky legal and taxation issues, and the rules frequently change—seemingly, whenever Uncle Sam wants a bigger piece of the tax pie. If you have substantial assets, it's prudent to have an attorney on board for at least part of the estate planning process. You should also consider bringing your financial planner into the loop. Many financial planners, particularly those who are also attorneys or accountants, specialize in estate planning issues (many will actually call themselves "estate planners" to make it clear where their specialty lies).

What You'll Learn in This Chapter:

▶ The basics of estate planning and how to determine whether you should hire an estate planning professional.

▶ How wills are set up.

▶ How sites can provide you with different tools to minimize the bite of estate taxes.

▶ How you can find additional help with the softer side of estate planning.

Bits and Bytes:

At the outset, remember this... Nothing can replace sitting down with a competent estate planning attorney to discuss your particular situation.

But the good news is that you can do some of the necessary estate planning nuts and bolts on your own. This is easier than ever thanks to the Internet's capability to educate, foster discussion, and disseminate information about wills, trusts, and other elements of estate planning. Indeed, hundreds of attorneys, accountants, financial planners, and other professionals who work in estate planning have put a lot of helpful resources on the Internet—many of them for free. There are many organizations that can lend assistance as well.

This chapter will look at some of the basics of estate planning and how you can find out more about them on the Internet. Because so much of estate planning is specific to personal circumstances, we can't go into too much detail on particular strategies that you should employ. It will really depend on variables such as your age, your tax bracket, the size of your estate, the state you live in, how many heirs you have, and so forth. We'll just try to point you in the right direction online.

The Basics

As with so many aspects of personal finance, a basic understanding of estate planning will go a long way toward better preparation. Estate planning confounds even some experts.

Overheard:

Estate planning will undergo a boom in the next decade, as $40 trillion gets passed from this generation to the next. According to the U.S. Census Bureau, the population aged 65 and older grew by 82% between 1965 and 1995.

You don't want to start out blind. As in so many other areas of personal finance, estate planning is full of salespeople eager to pitch you a product, whether it's a complicated trust or an expensive will that you really might not need. Many of these vendors have colonized the Internet with some pretty hard-sell sites.

Let's start by checking out some general Web sites where you may learn the basics of estate planning.

One of these sites is *http://www.savewealth.com*, which is run by a company called The Preservation Group. This Carlsbad, California firm sells estate planning tools, such as trusts and life insurance, but its site is set up more as a consumer education site than as a sales pitch.

Although it's a commercial site, SaveWealth.com offers lots of good consumer education on estate planning.

This site offers tax and retirement information as well as info on estate planning. From the home page, simply go to the olive-green navigation bar on the left and click on the very first item, Estate Planning. (For a shortcut, just go to *http://www. savewealth.com/planning/estate/index.html*.) This is the site's Guide to Estate Planning, with a list of specific topics and a nice clear introduction to why estate planning is so important and what the process entails. It's extremely easy to understand. Spend some quality time browsing from topic to topic at the Preservation Group site. You'll get a good sense of the breadth of this topic as you read about everything from taxes and wills to many different kinds of trusts.

Another site with similarly broad information on the myriad ins and outs of estate planning is run by Nolo Press at *http://www. nolo.com/encyclopedia/ep_ency.html*. This site bills itself as an encyclopedia for wills and estate planning, and it does contain volumes' worth of information on the subject. No wonder: Nolo Press is a respected publisher of self-help books and other materials on a variety of legal topics. Its site is a repository of much of this information, and it's free of charge. (As a visitor to the site, you'll be politely encouraged to buy a Nolo book on estate planning, but there's no obligation to do so.)

Nolo's site.

The site has clearly defined sections on general estate planning, wills, and *probate*—which is the legal process of validating your will and passing along any assets to your heirs. It also goes into some detail on powers of attorney—a transfer of legal authority over your assets from yourself to a designated person. For each of these areas, Nolo includes a list of FAQs, or frequently asked questions.

Because the Nolo site sells books offering legal assistance with wills and estate planning, its site is skewed just a bit toward do-it-yourselfers. We strongly suggest that you sit down with an estate planner before making any serious estate planning moves.

For example, if you have a large asset base—say, over $600,000 or $700,000—forget about handling estate planning all on your own. With that kind of money, you may face some fairly complicated taxation questions. Every estate gets a federal tax exemption up to the first $675,000 (for 2000 and 2001—it rises to $1 million in 2006), no questions asked. Above that level, some pretty hefty taxes start kicking in. The federal estate tax (also known as the death tax) starts at 37% and rises as high as 55%. It's not hard to see how a fairly nice home, a healthy IRA, pension benefits, and a good-sized life insurance policy can easily vault many people over the $675,000 limit. In such cases, calling in a pro to help fashion your estate plan could save you—or, really, your heirs—tens of thousands of dollars…maybe more!

There are other reasons for seeking professional estate planning assistance. If you're a business owner or have a business partner, you face complicated rules of transferring assets and ownership. If you're concerned that someone might contest your will—that is, dispute its provisions—you should get some advice ahead of time on will/trust preparation. If you're trying to make some fairly complicated plans for someone with special needs who you want to provide for after you die—a disabled son or daughter, for instance—it makes good sense to consult a pro.

An educational site run by the American Academy of Estate Planning Attorneys will quiz you on estate planning to see just where you stand on the skittish scale. Let's try it out just for fun.

1. Open your browser to *http://www.estateplanforyou.com/home.html*.

2. Scroll down the middle section, in white, to the heading labeled I.Q. Quiz. Click on that link.

3. Here you're quizzed on estate planning basics. No pressure, but take the quiz to see what you can learn. Start filling in your answers.

4. When you're finished, click on See Your Results at the bottom of the quiz. You get your score, along with an explanation of each correct answer.

▼ **Try It Yourself**

▲

This is a great way to learn about some critical issues of estate planning. For instance, the quiz covers the all-important estate tax exemption level you just learned about. (Bet you got that one right!)

Learning About Wills

Now let's look more closely at wills, which are among the most widely used estate planning tools. Just about everyone should write a will, although all too few of us actually get around to it.

Overheard:

Seventy percent of Americans die without having prepared a will, which is known as dying *intestate*. What a mistake! Many people assume that their assets will automatically go to a spouse, but they may be divided among spouses, siblings, and parents. Don't let your state make a will for you when you die! Take control now.

There's absolutely no good reason not to *at least* write a will. For most people it's not expensive. Even hiring an attorney to do one can cost well under $500, depending on its complexity. What's more, doing a will is simpler than you might think. Although it's certainly necessary to have a will, not all of your estate is distributed through it. If you're married, for instance, your spouse automatically receives full ownership of any jointly owned property, and thus the transfer of these assets doesn't depend on a will. If you've already named someone as the beneficiary of an IRA—say, your wife or son or daughter—that passes outside of your will as well, thus avoiding probate.

Not surprisingly, the Internet is full of resources specifically about wills. Many of them come from attorneys and estate planners eager to sell you on their will-writing services, and others come from services that will let you download a will template. As you might expect, such sites are proliferating as the demand for wills soars with America's aging population. But while some online hucksterism abounds, some of these sites are downright helpful background-wise, particularly if you've never seen or read a will before.

Along those lines, let's visit a site run by the law firm of Teahan & Constantino, which puts a sample will on its Web site for educational purposes.

Try It Yourself ▼

1. Open your browser to *http://www1.mhv.net/~teahan/samppla.htm.*

2. You see an outline in stark black and white (apparently, the law firm wasn't too concerned about aesthetics). Click on the second item, Sample Will for Married Testator with Children.

   Amongst the legalese, which is the real meat of the will, you'll see boldfaced lines that explain the document's various parts in plain English.

3. Scroll down to the will portion titled Residuary Estate. The boldfaced text explains various options for dealing with any other parts of this person's estate besides what has already been specified.

4. Keep on scrolling down to the end of the will. Each clause is explained in this manner, giving you a virtual tour through the will.

You can also learn more about wills and trusts by visiting some of the personal finance portal sites, such as Quicken.com. If you go over to *http://www.quicken.com/retirement/wills/*, an area of the site that deals with other aspects of estate planning, you'll be a few clicks away from many articles on wills and other estate planning topics.

Likewise, at *Money* magazine's site, *http://www.money.com*, you can find transcripts from live online chats with financial planners answering emailed questions about wills and trusts. To find these chats, start at Money's home page and scroll down to the very bottom, almost as far down as you can go, to the green link labeled Chat. Click on it, and then you'll have a choice of current MoneyLive chats on the left and archives on the right. Check the archives by scrolling down through the descriptions of previous chats.

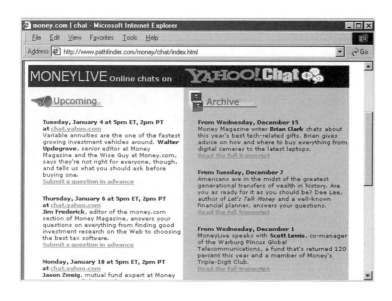

Yahoo! Chat offers a number of chat groups at the MoneyLive site.

Bits and Bytes:

The best use of this kind of site is to better familiarize yourself with the process, including forms, terms, and so on. We believe that wills and trusts should be drawn up by qualified lawyers.

Once you're somewhat familiar with wills and trusts—thanks to all these helpful sites—you will feel more comfortable when you

sit down with an estate planning professional. Although we don't
believe that you should write your own will, you might want to
look at the Web's plethora of will-writing services and download-
able wills. Let's visit a site called WillWorks for educational purposes.

*Although sites
like WillWorks
offer do-it-
yourself forms
and information,
we recommend
that you consult a
lawyer.*

Try It Yourself ▼

1. Open your browser to the site's home page at
   http://www.willworks.com.

2. At the top of the page is a horizontal black navigation bar,
   and the second item from the left is labeled Make My Will.
   Click on it.

3. You now see a page asking for your name, address, marital
   status, and whether you have any children. Fill out this information, and then click on the Continue to Page 2 of 5 button
   at the bottom. For the purposes of this example, let's say
   you're married with one child. Here's a nice touch: If at any
   point you don't understand why you're being asked something or exactly what WillWorks wants, you can click on the
   blue More Info button to have each question spelled out.

4. Now you're asked to name your spouse and your child, as
   well as provide your child's age. If your child is younger

than 18—for purposes of this example, let's say he is—writing a will is even more important. Having a child younger than 18 requires you, in most states, to name a guardian who can legally act in your place. Fill in this information and go on to the next page.

5. The next page updates this information and summarizes the kind of will you'll need. In this case, it's a simple will bequeathing just about everything to your spouse first, and then to your child if your spouse dies. The update also takes you to the next set of questions, in which you decide how to provide for guardianship, look at some options for passing on assets to your child, and choose an executor(s). Fill in these questions and keep going.

6. Now you're asked to make any specific bequests. You've already arranged to pass on the bulk of your estate to your spouse or child, but here's where you could specify that your stamp collection goes to your brother, for instance. Simply type in the item, the person who's getting it, and his location.

7. You're now asked to follow several steps: go back and verify all the information you entered, make any changes, and save your information.

Lawyers should create a document such as this, but it's great background information. (The more you know, the less money it will cost to have your lawyer explain it to you!)

How to Minimize Estate Taxes

Estate taxes can eat up a hefty portion of your hard earned cash—more than half of it, in some extreme cases—unless you take action to protect those assets. There are many different asset preservation strategies. No two estate plans are truly alike. Although the Internet can't design your estate plan for you, it gives you the tools that can help you figure out your exposure to estate taxes and subsequently start crafting a strategy with an attorney.

Is it any surprise that there are online calculators to help even with estate planning? EstateWeb.com, a site that specializes in estate planning issues, offers a basic estate tax estimator that will give you a quick general snapshot of what your heirs can expect to pay. Let's check it out.

EstateWeb has a very simple calculator to help you figure out what part of your estate will go to Uncle Sam.

Try It Yourself ▼

1. Open your browser to *http://www.estateweb.com/*.

2. Click on the Estate Tax Estimator link above the navigation bar.

3. This is a very simple calculator that asks you to estimate your current estate and your allowable deductions. Fill in this information. (If only all of the calculators covered in this book were this easy!)

   Voila! You have your results, showing an estimation of your estate, deductions, net estate, estate tax before credits, estimated federal taxes due upon death, and the percentage of your estate that would be lost to taxes—ouch! Forewarned is forearmed!

Obviously, *any* assets eaten by estate taxes will seem like too much. If your estate is above the $675,000 limit (for 2000 and

2001), it's smart for you to investigate some tax-reduction options. These options are best discussed with an estate planning attorney.

Now let's compare EstateWeb to another site that also offers an estate tax calculator. Check out the LifeNET site's estate planning area at *http://www.lifenet.com/estate.html* and click on the link at the top marked Estate Tax Calculator. This calculator asks you to enter more information. It's worth the effort because the material you type in will be broken out in ways that will be more understandable to you. For instance, instead of just asking for the total estimated estate, this calculator breaks the same question into five different lines, asking "What you will own when you die" and so on. This calculator shows the various elements of calculating estate taxes. It does the same thing with deductions, using a separate line for each one to illustrate how debts, funeral expenses, administrative expenses, marital deductions, and charitable gifts all figure into your tax picture.

When it's all said and done, you get results from LifeNET's calculator that are similar to the results you got from EstateWeb's. Both sites break out the total estate, total deductions, and estimated estate tax—as well as estimated attorneys' fees.

LifeNET offers you practical advice on minimizing Uncle Sam's tax bite.

Now that you know the awful truth—just how much Uncle Sam may want from your estate after your death—what can you do about it? There are many options, most of them in the estate planning area. Again, wills and trusts aren't just for the rich, despite their associations with yacht-sailing, champagne-swilling socialites. They're simply tools that many people use to minimize the tax bite on their estates.

You'll find a helpful list of some common trusts and other so-called wealth preservation tactics at the American Academy of Estate Planning Attorneys site at *http://www.estateplanforyou. com/home.html*. Just off its home page, this site lists and then defines the "Top 10 Planning Techniques." Here you'll find out about the very common $10,000 annual gift tax exclusion. You can give up to $10,000 a year as a gift, tax-free, to anyone—such as your children or grandchildren—thus reducing the taxable assets left in your estate.

At the American Academy of Estate Planning Attorneys site, you may find a lawyer near you who specializes in estate planning.

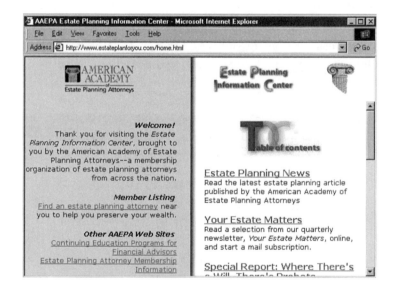

This site is a comprehensive introduction to the variety of trusts and other estate planning tools you may consider employing. You'll need to hire an estate planning attorney to discuss trusts and the like. They're just too complicated to attempt yourself. So how do you find someone who can help you fashion an estate plan?

Not all estate planning lawyer Web searches are alike. The one we found at EstateWeb was positively awful, turning up no matches at all for the entire state of Florida—which, given its huge senior-citizen population, is teeming with estate planners. But you'll get a good basic ZIP code–based search at *http://www. estateplanning.com*, a site run by Schumacher Publishing (which, like our old friends at Nolo Press, publishes estate planning books). The American Academy of Estate Planning Attorneys site also offers a search function.

Other Estate Planning Preparations

What about your loved ones, who'll actually have to deal with all of your estate matters when you're gone?

Not surprisingly, you'll find other estate planning assistance online as well. We're not talking about the legal stuff, such as the wills, the tax details, or the trusts, but rather the *softer* side of estate planning. This deals with surviving the first few confusing days after a loved one dies. You can make things a lot easier by ensuring that all your important documents are in the right place and your heirs know where everything is before you die.

You'll find materials such as this at, of all places, a vendor site run by Deloitte & Touche—a large accounting firm that offers estate planning services. Go to *http://www.dtonline.com/estate/ checklist.htm* to find a checklist of the steps you need to take shortly after a spouse dies and as estate plans start to unfold. To use the checklist, just print it out and fill it in.

Overheard:

A *living trust* is a type of estate planning tool that generally avoids probate. Not a bad idea, because probate costs, such as attorney and court fees, can range from 4% to 10% of your overall estate in some states. But avoidance of probate is only one of many reasons that a trust may make sense for you.

*Deloitte &
Touche's Web site
has a checklist of
what to do shortly
after a spouse
dies.*

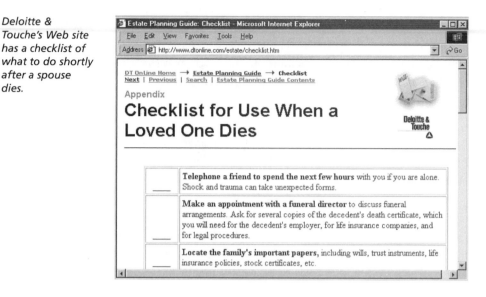

The site also has a very useful recordkeeping feature, which you
may also print out at home and, ideally, store in a fireproof box.
You'll find it by going to Deloitte & Touche's Estate Planning
Guide at *http://www.dtonline.com/estate/cover.htm*, scrolling to
the menu bar on the left, and choosing Recordkeeping. This is a
document that lists all your insurance policies, bank or brokerage
account numbers, other securities accounts, notes receivable, real
estate and car title information, and details on where your tax
returns and will may be found—even things such as where the
safe deposit box key is and how to access the box after you're
gone or where your marriage certificate or cemetery deeds are
stored. It's well worth having—and Deloitte & Touche is kind
enough to make it available for free to anyone visiting the site.

On Your Way

You've really just dipped your toe into the water—estate
planning–wise. It's among the most complicated areas of personal
finance. But now you're equipped with at least the basic knowledge to contact an estate planning attorney and get started.

- Smart estate planning is necessary for almost everyone, not
  just affluent people, in order to avoid excessive taxation and
  to ensure that your estate is properly settled when you're no
  longer around.

- There are a variety of estate planning tools available to help you minimize your estate taxes.

- Estate planning should extend beyond legal matters to areas such as recordkeeping.

- You should sit down and discuss your estate planning needs with a qualified attorney. Don't try to do it all on your own.

PART VI

Appendixes

APPENDIX A

Web Sites Worth Visiting

To save you surfing time, we've checked out a bunch of Web sites. Here are some of our favorites.

Chapter 1, "What Is Personal Finance?", and Chapter 2, "How Can I Use the Internet for Personal Finance?"

URL	Description
www.money.com	*Money* magazine's portal, offering a good personal finance overview.
www.smartmoney.com	*SmartMoney* magazine's portal, which includes access to SmartMoney University.
www.quicken.com	Home page for Quicken, best-selling software sold by Intuit Corp. Acts as a portal.
www.moneycentral.msn.com	Microsoft's MoneyCentral portal.
www.personalwealth.com	General finance information.
www.bankrate.com	Extremely helpful personal finance site.
www.university.smartmoney.com	SmartMoney University, where you can take free "courses" on investing and other topics.
www.greenmagazine.com	Green Magazine.com, an irreverent personal finance portal aimed at people in their 20s.
www.iionline.com	Individual Investor Online, an investing-oriented portal site.
www.quote.com	Quote.com, an investing-oriented portal and home of Quote.com University.
www.learn2.com	A site consisting of tutorials on various topics, including many financial ones.
www.financenter.com	A site full of free calculators for just about any purpose and comprehensive stock research.

Chapter 3, "Budgeting—Planning for Today and the Future"

URL	Description
www.aba.com/aba/ ConsumerConnection/CNC games.htm.	Quick budget game featuring "Penny Banks" as your MC.
www.smartmoney.com/ac/ estate/index.cfm?story=networth	SmartMoney's Net Worth calculator, letting you take stock of your red ink.
www.financenter.com/ budgeting.html	FinanCenter's budgeting calculator, showing how your debt affects your ability to save.
www.familymoney.com	Family Money magazine's home page, with links to budgeting resources and articles.
www.quicken.com	Quicken's home page, where you can link to its QuickAnswers calculators while using the budgeting software.

Chapter 4, "Banking Online—Managing Your Money over the Internet"

URL	Description
www.bankofamerica.com	Bank of America's home page, with a demo that shows how online banking works.
www.gomezadvisors.com www.gomez.com	Gomez Advisors' site, where you can access objective ratings of different online banks.
www.wingspanbank.com/ sessionManager/dispatch?service =BILLPAY	Wingspan Bank's demo for its bill payment service.
www.bankrate.com	Bankrate's interest rate comparisons and credit information.
www.rate.net	RateNet's interest rate comparisons.
www.banxquote.com	BanxQuote's interest rate comparisons.

Chapter 5, "Credit and Debt—Taking Care of Your Liabilities Using the Internet"

URL	Description
www.bankrate.com/brm/ ccstep.asp	Bankrate's tutorial on how credit cards work and the pros and cons of using them.
www.cardweb.com	CardWeb, a site that lets you compare various offers from different credit card issuers.
getoutofdebt.com	Credit help.
www.bankrate.com/brm/ green/perloan/perloan1a.asp	Primer on unsecured personal loans on Bankrate's site.
www.creditinfocenter.com/	The Credit Information Center, a clearinghouse for information on consumer credit and your rights as a borrower.
www.banksite.com	BankSite, which promises to email you a copy of your credit report in 30 seconds for $8.
www.credit411.com	Credit 411, which offers a selection of credit reports from three bureaus.
www.ivillagemoneylife. com/money/articles/ 0,4029,12462~365,00.html	iVillage's interactive debt reduction planner.
wellsfargo.com/per/ planner/debt/info/	The debt reduction planner created by Quicken and available on Wells Fargo Bank's site.
www.nfcc.org	The National Foundation for Consumer Credit's home page. Find a nonprofit credit counselor in your area.
www.getsmart.com/	Information on debt consolidation products and links to lenders on GetSmart's home page.

Chapter 6, "Insurance—Finding the Best Policy Online"

URL	Description
www.iii.org	Home page of the Insurance Information Institute, a good general source of background information on insurance.
www.acli.com	The American Council of Life Insurance's home page.
www.hiaa.org	The Health Insurance Association of America's home page.
www.independentagent.com/	IndependentAgent.com, where you can use the AgentLocator feature to find an insurance agent in your area.
www.insweb.com *www.quotesmith.com*	Two of the most comprehensive and useful insurance shopping sites.
longtermcareinsurance.org	Specializes in long-term care information.
www.weissratings.com	Check out an insurance company's financial stability.
www.insure.com	Insure.com, where you can check out whether an insurance company has run afoul of any regulations.
www.seniorresource.com/ insur.htm	Senior Resource's home page, with links to numerous articles on insurance products for the elderly.
www.johnhancock.com	John Hancock Insurance's home page.

Chapter 7, "Taxes—Internet Resources to Help You Keep More of Your Money"

URL	Description
www.smartmoney.com/ac/tax/	SmartMoney's tax primer, with archived and new articles on taxes.
www.fairmark/com/	The home page for Fairmark Press, chock-full of useful tax background information.

URL	Description
www.irs.gov/	The IRS home page, ground zero for downloading tax forms and tax publications, as well as getting other information on taxes and taxpaying.
www.quicken.com/taxes/	Quicken's tax area, with Investor Decision tax calculators to help you decide whether to sell or hold investments based on capital gains.
www.irs.gov/ elec_svs/elf-txpyr.html	The IRS's list of authorized e-filing providers.
www.trac.syr.edu/tracirs	Syracuse University's site for IRS audit information.
www.taxweb.com	TaxWeb, a site with answers to detailed tax questions and links to other tax-related Web sites.
www.intelligenttaxes.com	General tax information.
www.tax.org/	Home page for Tax Analysts Online, which can fill you in on where all your tax dollars actually go.
www.taxsites.com	Tax Sites, a directory of other tax sites on the Internet.
www.taxsites.com/ associations2.html#societies	Tax Sites' list of all 50 states' Certified Public Accountant societies, useful for locating a CPA near you.
www.accountant-search.com	Home page for Accountant-Search, another source for finding an accountant in your area.

Chapter 8, "Investing Online—Growing Your Nest Egg"

URL	Description
www.university. smartmoney.com/Departments/ Investing101/	SmartMoney University's Investing 101 introduction, listing all available courses.

continues

URL	Description
www.better-investing.org	Home page for the National Association of Investors Corp., the main organization for investment clubs.
www.sec.gov/mfcc/ mfcc-int.htm	The Securities and Exchange Commission's mutual fund cost calculator, useful for figuring out how expense ratios affect your funds' returns.
www.morningstar.com	Morningstar's home page, which allows you to screen mutual funds and get general fund information.
www.fundalarm.com	FundAlarm.com, which contains the list of Three-Alarm Funds that lag behind their benchmarks in terms of performance.
www.ici.org/	Home page of the Investment Company Institute, the mutual fund industry's main trade organization.
www.sec.gov/oiea1.htm	The SEC site's Office of Investor Education and Advice area, with instructions on using Edgar and other resources.
moneycentral.msn.com/ investor/research/wizards/ SRW.asp	MSN MoneyCentral's Research Wizard feature, which helps you research stocks by walking you through each element of stock analysis.
www.cnbc.com	CNBC's home page, useful for financial news and commentary.
cbs.marketwatch.com	CBS MarketWatch's home page, a site owned by CBS and set up specifically for financial news.
www.hoovers.com	Hoover's Online, where you can search for basic, unbiased background information on thousands of public and private companies. There's a fee for some information.
www.gomezadvisors.com www.gomez.com	Gomez Advisors' home page, which ranks online brokerages according to various criteria.

URL	Description
www.ameritrade.com	Ameritrade, a large online broker, where you can conduct a demo and see what it's like to trade online.
www.investinginbonds.com	Home page for the Bond Association of America, useful for obtaining basic background information on bonds.
www.ragingbull.com	Raging Bull, one of the major investing message boards.

Chapter 9, "Family Finances—Your Changing Needs as Your Family Grows"

URL	Description
www.metlife.com/	Metropolitan Life Insurance's LifeAdvice Center, which offers tips and guidance on how various life events affect your financial picture.
www.loveathome.com/	Love at Home, a family lifestyle-oriented site that also features a number of financial articles in its Columns and Family Finance areas.
www.excite.com/family/ family_planning/ family_finance/	Excite.com is a search engine, but this area of the site, called the Family Finance search, lists various family-oriented financial sites.
www.ivillagemoneylife.com	iVillage's MoneyLife section, with articles and background on determining your future spouse's attitudes toward money and spending.
www.ivillagemoneylife. com/money/quiz/ 0,4055,12471~356,00.html	A MoneyStyles quiz to help you go one step further toward figuring out your partner's approach to money.
www.theknot.com	The Knot.com, a wedding site that features a wedding calculator.
www.infostuff.com/weddings	This general informational site's weddings area tells you where your money goes for a typical wedding.

continues

URL	Description
www.bankrate.com/brm/ prenup.asp	Bankrate's brief introduction to prenuptial agreements.
www.babycenter.com	At BabyCenter, a site mainly for new parents and parents-to-be, you can find content about budgeting for a new baby.
napfa.com	Financial planner information.
www.icfp.org	Financial planner information.
www.cfp-board.org	Financial planner information.
www.ivillagemoneylife. com/money/life_stage/ coupleskids/	The iVillage MoneyLife section's articles on talking to your children about money and budgeting.
www.divorcesource.com	Home page for Divorce Source, a site that helps newly divorced and separated people develop a fresh approach to their finances.
www.divorcesource.com/ archives/financial.shtml	Worksheets and articles on financial topics for divorced people.
divorcesupport.com	Divorce support for men and women.
www.ka-ching.com	Articles on how widows and widowers can approach family finances.

Chapter 10, "Real Estate—Buying and Selling Online"

URL	Description
www.relocationcentral.com	Relocation Central, a site that gives you information about cities and other areas where you could relocate.
www.virtualrelocation.com	Virtual Relocation, which allows you to run detailed side-by-side comparisons of different cities and towns.

URL	Description
www.pathfinder.com/ money/depts/real_estate/ bestplaces/	*Money* magazine's annual ratings of the best places to live in the United States, which you can search according to criteria that you deem important.
www.homefair.com/usr/ qualcalcform.html	Home-buying calculator offered by Homefair, which helps you assess how large a mortgage you can take on.
www1.countrywide.com/ Calculators/default.asp	Countrywide Home Loans' mortgage calculator.
www.interest.com	Mortgage.Interest.com, an online offshoot of Mortgage Market Information Services Mortgage Guide. This is a good general site for basic mortgage data.
www.hsh.com	Consumer loan information.
mortgagebot.com/	Home page for MortgageBot, which sells mortgages online.
www.realtor.com	Realtor.com, where you can search thousands of home listings across the country.
agentscout.com	Home page for AgentScout, which can match you up with a local real estate agent it has screened.
www.freddiemac.com	Home page for Freddie Mac, the Federal Home Loan Mortgage Corp. This site includes a kit for inspecting a home yourself and other home-buying resources.
www.ashi.com	The American Society of Home Inspectors' site, where you can enter your ZIP code to find a professional home inspector in your area.
db.legal.net/ldn/welcome/ query.cfm	At Legal.Net, an organization of attorneys, you can find a lawyer in your area who handles real estate closings.

Chapter 11, "College—Covering the Skyrocketing Costs of Higher Education"

URL	Description
www.usnews.com	Home page of *U.S. News and World Report*, which runs an annual rating of colleges in the United States. The site includes calculators to help you determine college costs.
www.salliemae.com	Sallie Mae, or the Student Loan Marketing Association, will let you download the CollegeCalc software to figure college costs and your contributions.
www.moneycentral.com	At MSN MoneyCentral, you can follow the Family & College heading to a useful Q&A section on paying for college.
www.collegesavings.org	This site, run by the College Savings Plan Network, tells you about state-sponsored college savings plans.
www.nasfaa.org	Home page of the National Association of Student Financial Aid Administrators, which is well-organized and full of useful information.
www.finaid.com	FinAid is a general financial aid information site, with separate areas for students, parents, and counselors.
www.fafsa.ed.gov	Main site for the government's Federal Student Financial Assistance program, where you can also download and fill out the ubiquitous FAFSA form.
www.collegeboard.org	Home page of the College Board, a site that acts as an overall college planner and offers useful scholarship searches.
www.fresch.org	Fresch, a site with attitude that your college-age kids might find fun to use for scholarship searches.
www.familymoney.com	Family Money's semester budget worksheet for college kids.

URL	Description
www.estudentloan.com	eStudentLoan.com lets you search among lenders for various student loans.
www.collegeparents.org	Home page of College Parents of America, an organization for anyone who's sending their kids to school and needs some company.

Chapter 12, "Retirement—Planning and Financing Your Golden Years"

URL	Definition
www.quicken.com/retirement	Quicken's retirement area, which is loaded with tools, links, searches, tips, and a section titled "Retirement Basics."
www.asec.org	Home page of the American Savings Education Council, where you can fill out a ballpark estimator to see how financially ready you are for retirement.
www.thirdage.com	Third Age, a site for people over 45, includes a host of retirement resources.
www.retireplan.about. com/finance/retireplan/ mbody.htm	At About.com's retirement area, you can link to dozens of sites about retirement (although many of them are vendor-oriented).
www.fool.com/Money/ AllAboutIRAs/AllAboutIRAs.htm	The Motley Fool's IRA primer, which includes IRA calculators and definitions of different types of IRAs.
www.thirdage.com/features/ money/ira/withdrawal.html	Third Age's calculator for determining minimum IRA withdrawals.
www.401kafe.com	Home page of the 401Kafe, a community-oriented site for anyone participating in a 401(k) plan.

continues

URL	Description
www.valic.com/valic/valweb.nsf	Valic's RetireNet site, a useful general information site on retirement plans and other financial aspects of retirement.
www.planningpaysoff.org/	Web site run by the International Association for Financial Planners, where you can search a database of financial planners in your area.
www.cfp-board.org	Home page for the Certified Financial Planners Board of Standards, where you can determine if a CFP has incurred any disciplinary actions.

Chapter 13, "Wills and Estate Planning— Taking Care of Your Heirs"

URL	Description
www.savewealth.com	Home page for The Preservation Group, a financial planning firm, and a good general source of estate planning information.
www.nolo.com/encyclopedia/ ep_ency.html	Nolo Press's estate planning encyclopedia, chock-full of definitions and explanations of complex estate planning tools.
www.estateplanforyou. com/home.html	Consumer education site run by the American Academy of Estate Planning Attorneys, which features an interactive quiz on estate planning and a top 10 list of popular estate planning tools.
www1.mhv.net/~teahan/ samppla.htm	Educational sample will offered by the Poughkeepsie, NY law firm of Teahan & Constantino.
www.quicken.com/retirement/ wills	General information on estate planning and wills at Quicken.com's site.

URL	Description
www.money.com	*Money* magazine's home page, from which you can search for archives of live chats with estate planners.
www.willworks.com	WillWorks, a site that sells interactive online wills.
www.estateweb.com/	A straightforward, bare-bones estate tax calculator at EstateWeb.com.
www.lifenet.com/estate.html	A complex yet easy-to-understand estate tax calculator at LifeNet.com.
www.estateplanning.com	Search engine for estate planning attorneys in the United States, offered by Schumacher Publishing.
www.dtonline/estate/cover.htm	Deloitte & Touche's estate planning area, where you'll find a free downloadable checklist and recordkeeping document.

APPENDIX B

Glossary

401(k) A retirement plan offered by private sector employers that allows employees to make tax-deferred salary contributions. This lowers their taxable income in the near term and allows those contributions to grow, tax-deferred, over the long term.

403(b) A retirement plan similar to a 401(k) plan but offered by public-sector employers, agencies, and nonprofit organizations.

account nickname A name applied to your online bank or brokerage account that makes it easier and faster for you to remember how to access your account.

annuity A tax-deferred investment sold by insurance companies, typically used for retirement planning.

ask price The price at which a security—such as a stock—is available for sale.

asset allocation The practice of dividing, or allocating, your investment dollars among different financial classes to better manage the risks of investing. A typical asset allocation plan will invest some money in stocks, some in bonds, and some in a money-market fund or cash.

audit An examination of your tax returns, documents, and records to see if you've underpaid any taxes.

back-end load A commission charged by a mutual fund when you sell shares of the fund.

benchmark In investing, a method of comparing the performance of one investment to another that's similar in some way. For instance, you might benchmark one oil company's stock against another oil company's stock.

beneficiary The person to whom assets, including those in a retirement account such as an IRA, are left upon the asset holder's death. Typically, you name beneficiaries in a will or trust.

bid price   The price that a buyer of a security is willing to pay for shares.

bond   A security that represents debt. As a bondholder, you're essentially lending money to the bond issuer. In return, the issuer promises to pay you back that money plus interest by a certain predetermined date or *maturity*.

bond fund   A mutual fund that will buy, sell, and hold only bonds in its portfolio.

brokerage firm   A firm where you can set up an account to buy and sell securities. Some banks have brokerage firm subsidiaries. Some brokerage firms operate only on the Internet. Others are brick-and-mortar firms that also operate online.

budget   A system of managing your income and expenses.

calculator   An online tool that helps you calculate and evaluate how a particular financial decision, situation, investment, or other scenario might affect your finances.

capital gains tax   The tax you must pay when you make a profit by either investing or selling an asset.

certified financial planner   A designation for a professional who has passed a series of exams and agreed to a code of ethics administered by the Certified Financial Planner Board of Standards. A CFP may also be an attorney, accountant, stockbroker, insurance salesperson, or other professional.

certified public accountant   A tax professional designation applied to someone who has passed a series of exams and agreed to a code of ethics.

chat room   A virtual space on the Internet in which users can exchange typed messages in real-time that anyone in the room can read. Many investment sites feature chat rooms where users discuss stocks, other investments, and the day's financial news.

claim   In insurance, the monetary amount that policyholders ask to be paid for damage to a home, car, or other property, or, in the case of life insurance, if they die.

community bank   A small bank that serves a particular town or community, accepting deposits from individuals and small businesses, making loans, and originating mortgages.

community site A Web site that is directed toward users with a common interest or goal. Community sites are typically centered around message boards, chat rooms, and news and information.

corporate filing Reports that all public companies must file with the Securities and Exchange Commission on a quarterly basis, as well as before initially going public, merging with another company, or conducting certain other business. Corporate filings are public information that may be accessed online via the SEC's Edgar system (see Edgar).

credit Access to loans, such as those offered via credit cards or mortgages, that are extended along with an interest rate. Usually, the higher the risk that the lender takes on, the higher the interest rate it charges.

credit bureau A company that keeps a record of your credit history and provides this data to lenders and other organizations. The Fair Credit Reporting Act gives you the legal right to see the information a credit bureau is sending out about you and to have any errors corrected.

credit card An extension of a line of credit, represented by a card that you can use for virtually any purpose at a variety of retailers and other merchants. Most credit cards are unsecured, which means you don't need any collateral to obtain them.

credit report A document showing your past credit history, such as loans you've been given, outstanding debts (including credit card debts), how promptly you've made payments, and any collection activities that have been taken against you. Under the Fair Credit Reporting Act, you have a legal right to know what's in your credit report and to fix any errors that might be there.

creditor Any person or institution that has lent money to a borrower.

debt Generally speaking, money owed as the result of credit that was extended.

debt consolidation The practice of paying down one's debt by combining many different debts into one payment, which is usually at a lower interest rate than those originally used.

debtor   Anyone who owes money and has agreed to pay it back to a creditor.

disclosure   The release by all public companies of any information, good or bad, that affects investors.

discount brokerage   A brokerage firm that typically just accepts orders to buy and sell securities without offering specific advice or counsel to its clients. In exchange, they get a commission that's often 50% to 75% cheaper than the commissions charged by a full-service brokerage firm.

due diligence   Researching and checking a financial company's background to ensure that it's on sound financial footing.

Edgar   The acronym for Electronic Data Gathering Analysis and Retrieval, an online service of the Securities and Exchange Commission. By using Edgar, you can access public corporate filings.

e-filing   A method of filing taxes online using the Internal Revenue Service's approved list of e-filing companies. e-Filing is considerably faster than traditional tax filing, according to the IRS.

equity   In investing, a synonym for stock. In real estate, your share of the value of a property. If you have 50% equity in a home, for instance, you own exactly half of that home.

estate planning   An overall plan that organizes the disposition of your assets, including real estate, investments, and life insurance.

executor   An individual appointed by you in your will, or by the court if you die intestate, who is responsible for the disposition of your assets.

expense ratio   A figure that tells you how expensive a mutual fund is to own. An expense ratio consists of a fund's management, administrative, and marketing fees, as well as any sales loads.

FAFSA The standard Free Application for Federal Student Aid form, which students fill out to determine their eligibility for such aid based on their own and their parents' financial status.

Fair Credit Reporting Act A federal law that gives you the right to see your credit report and to have any errors corrected.

Fannie Mae The Federal National Mortgage Association, which is a government lending agency that helps first-time homebuyers qualify for mortgages, as well as other types of borrowers.

financial aid Any kind of financial assistance with college tuition and other expenses.

fixed expense An expense in your household budget that doesn't fluctuate from month to month or week to week, such as a mortgage payment.

flexible expense An expense in your household budget that can fluctuate from month to month or over any given time period, such as clothing or entertainment expenses.

Freddie Mac The Federal Home Loan Mortgage Corporation, which buys mortgages from banks and other companies that originate the loans and then resells them as securities.

front-end load A commission charged by a mutual fund when you purchase shares of the fund.

full-service brokerage A brokerage firm that, in addition to buying and selling securities, offers a wide range of products and services in exchange for a commission.

fundamentals The most basic elements of stock research, consisting of a company's balance sheet: its earnings, assets, income, sales, debts, management team, and so forth.

gift tax exclusion A tax exclusion that allows you to give an unlimited number of gifts, up to $10,000 a year, to any number of individuals completely tax-free.

home equity line of credit A line-of-credit loan made to a homeowner, with the home secured as collateral, that may be tapped for purposes ranging from debt consolidation to home improvements. Once a homeowner uses this line of credit, a lien is imposed on the home that must be paid back before selling it.

home inspector   A professional you hire to analyze and inspect a home, prior to either buying it or selling it, to determine its condition and point out any flaws or problems.

hybrid fund   A mutual fund that may own both stocks and bonds. Some hybrid funds are also called balanced funds.

insurance quote   The premium cost you're given for a particular insurance policy prior to actually purchasing it, based on your personal information and other kinds of data you supply to the insurer.

insurance rating   A rating, usually represented as a letter grade such as AAA or AA, that's given to an insurance company by an independent rating company based on the company's financial soundness.

interest rate   The rate at which you may borrow money, such as for a mortgage or home equity line of credit. Interest rates are determined by lenders such as banks, which base them on the prevailing interest rates set by the Federal Reserve. A high interest rate means it's more costly to borrow money; a low interest rate means it's cheaper.

Internet-only bank   A bank that operates solely over the Internet, as opposed to a brick-and-mortar branch. Internet-only banks must conduct some business, such as deposits, via regular mail.

intestate   To die without leaving a will. In such a case, the state determines who will inherit your assets.

investing   The practice of buying/selling an investment with the objective of seeing your assets grow over time.

investment club   An organized group that pools its money and invests in stocks, bonds, and other securities together by delegating research, appointing club officers, and meeting at set times to vote on and discuss its portfolio.

IRA (Individual Retirement Account)   A common account used to defer taxes on money saved for retirement. Assets deposited into an IRA are tax-deferred until you begin to withdraw them. An individual can deposit up to $2,000 a year into an IRA, or a couple may deposit up to $4,000 a year. IRA accountholders must pay a penalty if they withdraw any of the money before age 59 and a half.

irrevocable trust   A trust that cannot be terminated by you. Most often used for making gifts or establishing a permanent arrangement for the benefit of your family or favorite charities.

Keogh plan   A tax-deferred retirement plan available to the self-employed.

limit order   An order to buy or sell stock at a specific price or better. This is often a safer way to trade online than with a market order. If there are any electronic delays in your trade's execution, you won't pay more than you expected if the stock's price goes up by the time your trade goes through.

living trust   A trust you create and control while you're alive, usually designed to avoid probate and/or reduce estate taxes.

living will   A document that explains in writing what medical treatments you want to receive in case of terminal illness. A living will takes effect only when you're unable to directly communicate your wishes.

load   A sales commission or sales fee attached to a mutual fund that applies either when purchasing the fund, as a front-end load, or when selling it, as a back-end load.

long-term capital gains   The profits from the sale of a security that you have owned for more than one year. The rate of taxation on long-term capital gains is less than that of short-term capital gains.

market order   An order to buy or sell stock at the best available price at the time the order is entered.

matching contribution   A sum of money that your employer contributes to your retirement account matching a sum of money that you contribute yourself.

message board   An online bulletin board that allows users to post messages on various topics, to which other users can then respond. Most message boards are organized by topic, or thread, to keep them manageable.

minimum withdrawal   Withdrawals from an IRA that you're legally required to make starting no later than the April after you turn 70 and a half.

money center bank   A very large bank that operates worldwide and plays a major role as a lender to large corporations and governments. Many money center banks also serve individual retail customers as well.

mutual fund   An investment company that pools its shareholders' money and invests it in a portfolio of stocks, bonds, and other securities.

net worth   The total value of all your assets, minus any outstanding debts (liabilities).

no-load   A mutual fund sold with no sales commission or fee. Some no-load funds have lower expense ratios than load funds, although this is not guaranteed.

nonconforming loan   A real estate loan that does not meet the guidelines established by the quasi-government agencies Fannie Mae (FNMA) and Freddie Mac (FHLMC). Generally, these loans are made by investors and have higher interest rates.

pension plan   An investment plan offered by an employer that sets aside assets for use during retirement.

personal loan   A loan extended to you by a bank or other lender for virtually any purpose.

point   A fee charged by a lender, usually a mortgage lender, at the time the loan is made. One point represents 1% of the loan's value. On a $100,000 mortgage, two points would be $2,000.

portal   A Web site that acts as a gateway to topics and typically offers many links to other Web sites. Many portals act as authorities on particular topics, presenting news, commentary, analysis, calculators, statistics, and other resources.

portfolio   A collection of securities held by an individual or group.

pre-approval   A guarantee from a mortgage lender that you qualify for a mortgage based on financial data you've already supplied to the lender. Usually, a pre-approval expires after a set period of time.

premium   The fee you must pay regularly to an insurance company to maintain your policy and insurance protection.

prequalification   An indication from a mortgage lender that you've applied for a mortgage but have not yet been approved. Pre-qualification carries less weight than pre-approval, and it's no guarantee that you'll be able to obtain a mortgage.

price history   An aspect of stock research, based on analyzing a stock's previous price in order to evaluate if its current price is relatively expensive or inexpensive.

price target   A part of the stock research process in which you look at the expected price a stock will reach (set by professional analysts) over a given period of time, compared to the stock's current price.

private mortgage insurance   A type of insurance usually required by mortgage lenders for any borrower who can't put up at least a 20% down payment on a home. PMI, as it's called, is combined with the monthly mortgage payment. It should be eliminated when the homeowner's equity reaches 22%.

probate   The legal process by which a court administers a deceased person's estate. This process includes appointing an executor, settling accounts with creditors and debtors, and distributing the assets to heirs.

prospectus   A document that must be sent to every prospective mutual fund shareholder by the fund company. It explains the fund's goals, investment methods and objectives, expenses, and management fees.

regional bank   A mid-sized or large bank that operates in a number of states, with separate units in each state. Most regional banks conduct a mix of corporate and retail business with individuals.

Sallie Mae The Student Loan Marketing Association, which guarantees student loans and purchases them from originating lenders such as banks. Sallie Mae also provides financing to state student loan agencies.

screening engine An online method of narrowing down the field of potential fund or stock investments according to certain criteria that you input. You type in the desired parameters, and the screening engine eliminates all investments that don't meet those parameters.

secured credit Any kind of credit or loan that's backed up by collateral, such as your home.

Securities and Exchange Commission (SEC) The government agency charged with oversight over the United States stock exchanges, brokerage firms, and all other aspects of the securities markets.

security A financial instrument such as a stock, bond, or mutual fund that denotes either an ownership role (as in a stock or fund) or a creditor role (as in a bond). When investing, you buy, sell, and hold securities.

SEP Acronym for Simplified Employee Pension plan. A SEP is often used by self-employed people and independent contractors.

short-term capital gains The profits from the sale of securities that you've owned for less than one year. The rate of taxation is higher on short-term capital gains than on long-term ones.

state insurance department An agency administered by each state that is charged with setting the state's insurance rules and regulations, and with overseeing insurance companies licensed in that state.

stock Ownership in a publicly traded or private company. Each unit of ownership is represented as a share. Stockholders have the right to know about a company's financial dealings and other business, and also to vote for the company's board of directors. In order to buy and sell publicly traded stocks, you must open a brokerage account. Stocks are also known as equities.

stock fund A mutual fund that owns stocks, rather than bonds or other securities. A stock fund may also be called an equity fund.

stock quote   The price of a particular share of stock at a given time.

stock research   Analyzing a stock before buying or selling it. Typically, stock research involves studying not just a particular company, but also its industry and the stock market in general at a given point. Good stock research looks at historical data, both fundamental and technical, on the assumption that what has happened in the past to a certain company or industry, or to the market, can help predict what might happen in the future.

superregional bank   A very large bank that operates in many states across several regions, often from coast-to-coast.

tax form   A form used to file taxes. Federal tax forms are standard forms issued by the Internal Revenue Service; state tax forms are standard forms issued by each state's tax department. Many tax forms may be downloaded from the Internet.

tax-deferred retirement plan   Any kind of retirement plan, such as an IRA, 401(k), or 403(b), that allows you to invest money now on a tax-deferred basis and pay taxes on it during retirement when you withdraw the assets.

ticker symbol   A series of letters used to denote a specific stock or mutual fund.

trade   The practice of buying or selling a security.

transaction history   A record of all your transactions with a given bank or brokerage account, such as credits, debits, trades, and withdrawals.

transaction site   A Web site that allows its users to conduct financial transactions, such as trading stocks or paying bills.

trust   A legal arrangement by which one or more persons (the trustees) take control of assets and manage them for the benefit of another person (the beneficiary).

underwriting   In insurance, assessing a prospective policyholder's risk and then pricing (or *quoting*) the insurance policy premium according to that risk.

university site   A Web site that offers a wide range of virtual courses on a particular topic, such as investing or taxes.

unsecured credit   Any kind of credit or loan that isn't backed by collateral, such as with most credit cards. Because there's no collateral, unsecured credit usually comes with higher interest rates to compensate the lender for the risk of the borrower defaulting on the loan.

vendor site   A Web site that's run by a vendor of commercial products, such as insurance, securities, or mortgages. A vendor site's primary purpose is to actively sell or push its product, rather than to educate its users.

will   A legal declaration (usually written) stating your wishes for the disposition of your assets after you die.

INDEX

Symbols

401(k) plans, 18, 175-176
403(b) plans, 175

A

Accountant-Search Web site, 89
accountants, finding, 88
    Accountant-Search Web
    site, 89
    California Society of
    CPAs, 88
    Tax Sites Web site, 88
accounts, nicknames, 38
American Academy of Estate
    Planning Attorneys Web
    site, 192
American Bankers Association
    Web site, 29
American Council of Life
    Insurance Web site, 65
American Savings Education
    Council Web site, 170
applying for
    financial aid, 157
    mortgages, 135-136, 139-141
audits (tax), Syracuse University
    Web site, 86

B

Bank of America Web site, 37
    account nicknames, 38
    account services, 38

banking online, 35-39
    account services, 38
    Bank of America Web
    site, 37
        account nicknames, 38
    Gomez Advisors Web site
        bank ratings, 40
        comparing banks, 40
        consumer reviews, 40
        researching banks, 39
    interest rates, searching,
    44-45
    paying bills, 41-44
Bankrate Web site, 51
bills, paying, 41-44
bonds, 110
budgets, 27-29
    calculating net worth, 29-30
    creating, 28
    discussion groups, 33
    family finances
        new baby arrival,
        121-122
        single parenting,
        124-126
        weddings, 120
        young children, 123
    Family Money magazine Web
    site, 33
    financial calculators, 30-34
    software, Quicken, 33
buying real estate, 142-148

C

calculating
    college costs, 153
    net worth, 29-30

calculators, 22-23
  budgets, 30-34
  mortgages, 133-135
  mutual funds, 97-98
  taxes, 85
California Society of CPAs Web
  site, 88
CBS MarketWatch Web site, 106
College Board Web site, 158
College Parents of America Web
  site, 163
College Savings Plan Network
  Web site, 154
colleges, 149
  estimation of costs, 150-152
  saving for, 153-154
    financial aid, 155-157
    scholarships, 157-159
    state-run plans, 154
    student loans, 160-163
community sites
  401(k) plans, 18
  searching, 18
comparing
  banks, 40
  mortgages, 137-139
  scholarships, 159
Consumer Credit Counseling
  Services (CCCS), 52
Countrywide Home Loans Web
  site, 134
creating budgets, 28
credit, 47-48
  Consumer Credit Counseling
    Services (CCCS), 52
  credit card rates, 49
    message boards, 50
  credit reports, 51-54
  Fair Credit Reporting Act
    (FCRA), 52
    unsecured loans, 50
Credit Information Center Web
  site, 52

D

debt, 47-48, 54
  consolidation plans, 57-58
  debt reduction planning, 56
    iVillage Web site,
      54-56
    Quicken, 56
  National Foundation for
    Consumer Credit
    (NFCC), 57
Deloitte & Touche Web site, 193
deploying your cash, 7
disclosure, defined, 10
diversification (mutual funds), 96
DivorceSource Web site, 125
downloading tax forms, 81-82

E

E*Trade Web site, 21
electronic filing (taxes), 86
estate planning, 181-189
  American Academy of Estate
    Planning Attorneys, 192
  chat rooms, 187
  Deloitte & Touche Web
    site, 193
  estate planning quiz, 185
  LifeNet Web site, 191
  living trusts, 193
  Nolo Press Web site, 183
  powers of attorney, 184
  probate, 184
  Quicken Web site, 187
  SaveWealth Web site, 182
  taxes, 189-192
  WillWorks Web site, 188
eStudentLoan Web site, 161
expense ratios, mutual funds,
  96-97

F

Fair Credit Reporting Act
  (FCRA), 52
Fairmark Press Web site, 79
  Roth IRAs, 79
family finances, 117-120
  Family Money Web site, 123
  iVillage Money Styles
    quiz, 120
  Life Advice Library Web
    site, 118
  Love At Home Web site, 118
  message boards, 119
  new baby budgets, 121-122
  single parenting, 124-126
  wedding budgets, 120
  young children, 123
Family Money magazine Web
  site, 33, 123
financial aid
  applying for, 157
  college, 155-156
forms (tax), downloading, 81-82
FundAlarm Web site, 101

G

Gomez Advisors Web site
  bank ratings, 40
  comparing banks, 40
  consumer reviews, 40
  researching banks, 39
Green Web site, 20

H

Homefair Web site, 133
Hoover's Online Web site, 107

I-K

Independent Insurance Agents of
  America Web site, 66
insurance, 63-65
  American Council of Life
    Insurance, 65
  Insurance Information
    Institute Web site, 64
  Money magazine, 11
  purchasing, 73-75
  quotes, 66-69
    Independent Insurance
      Agents of America
      Web site, 66
  ratings, 70-72
    Insurance News
      Network, 72-73
    Senior Resource Web
      site, 73
interest rates, searching, 44-45
Internal Revenue Service (IRS)
  Web site, 80
Internet
  Money magazine
    insurance, 11
    investing, 10
    markets and news, 9-10
    real estate, 10
    taxes, 11
    Web site, 8
  personal finance, 13
  portals, 14-15
investments, 91-93
  bonds, 110
  chat rooms, 111
  investment clubs, 95
  message boards, 111
  Money magazine, 10

mutual funds, 94-99
    back-end loads, 99
    diversification, 96
    expense ratios, 96-97
    front-end loads, 99
    Morningstar Web
        site, 99
    online calculators,
        97-98
    Quick Take reports,
        100
    searching, 99-102
setting up, 95
stock
    CBS MarketWatch Web
        site, 106
    news sites, 106
    researching, 103-105
    trading, 107-110
IRAs (individual retirement
    accounts), 173-175
iVillage Web site, debt reduction
    planning, 54-56

Keogh plan (retirement), 169

L

Life Advice Library Web site, 118
LifeNet Web site, 191
loans
    for college, 160-163
    unsecured, 50
LoanWeb Web site, 138
long-term gains, 83
Love At Home Web site, 118

M

MetLife Web site, 23
Money magazine
    help categories, 8
    insurance, 11

investing, 10
markets and news, 9-10
real estate, 10
taxes, 11
Money magazine Web site, 8
Morningstar Web site, 99
Mortgagebot Web site, 140
mortgages
    applying for, 135-136,
        139-141
    calculating, 133-135
    comparing, 137-139
MSN MoneyCentral Web site, 15
Mutual Fund Connection Web
    site, 102
mutual funds, 94-99
    back-end loads, 99
    diversification, 96
    expense ratios, 96-97
    front-end loads, 99
    Morningstar Web site, 99
    online calculators, 97-98
    Quick Take reports, 100
    searching, 99-102

N

National Association Investors
    Corporation Web site, 95
National Association of Student
    Financial Aid Administrators
    Web site, 155
National Foundation for
    Consumer Credit (NFCC), 57
net worth, calculating, 29-30
news, *Money* magazine, 9-10
Nolo Press Web site, 183

O

online banking, 35-39
    account services, 38
    Bank of America Web
        site, 37
            account nicknames, 38

bills, paying 41-44
Gomez Advisors Web site
   bank ratings, 40
   comparing banks, 40
   consumer reviews, 40
   interest rates, 44-45
   researching banks, 39

P

paying bills, 41-44
personal finance
   budgets, 27-29
      calculating net worth,
        30
      creating, 28
      discussion groups, 33
      Family Money maga-
        zine Web site, 33
      financial calculators,
        30-32, 34
      software, 33
   calculating net worth, 29
   defined, 7
   deploying your cash, 7
   Internet, 13
   portals, 14-15
Pimco Innovation Fund Web
  site, 101
portals, 15
   calculators, 22-23
   defined, 14
   MSN MoneyCentral, 15-17
   searching topics, 17
      community sites, 18
      transaction sites, 21-22
      university sites, 18-20
      vendor sites, 23
purchasing
   insurance, 73-75
   real estate, 142-146

Q

Quick Take reports, 100
Quicken (software)
   budgeting, 33
   debt reduction planning, 56
Quicken Web site, 34, 169

R

Raging Bull Web site, 111
real estate, 127-129
   buying, 142-148
   city comparisons, 131-132
   Money magazine, 10
   mortgages
      applying for, 135-136,
        139-141
      calculators, 133-135
      comparing, 137-139
   purchasing, 148
   relocating, 129-130
   selling, 142-148
   viewing, 142-145
Relocation Central Web site, 129
researching
   bonds, 110
   stock, 103-105
      catalysts, 104
      comparisons, 104
      fundamentals, 104
      price history, 104
      price target, 104
retirement, 167-168, 172
   401(k) plans, 175-176
   403(b) plans, 175
   estimation of costs, 171
   financial planners/advisors,
     177-179
   IRAs (individual retirement
     accounts), 173-175
   Keogh plan, 169

Retirement Readiness Rating
quiz, 171
RetireNet Web site, 177
Roth IRAs, Fairmark Press Web
site, 79

S

SaveWealth Web site, 182
saving for college, 153-154
    financial aid, 155-157
    scholarships, 157-159
    state-run plans, 154
    student loans, 160-163
searching
    accountants, 88
        Accountant-Search
        Web site, 89
        California Society of
        CPAs, 88
        Tax Sites Web site, 88
    community sites, 18
    credit card rates, 49-50
    insurance quotes, 66-69
    interest rates, 44-45
    mutual funds, 99-102
    real estate, 129-130
    transaction sites, 21-22
    university sites, 18-20
    vendor sites, 23
selling real estate, 142-148
Senior Resource Web site, 73
setting up investment clubs, 95
short-term gains, 83
SmartMoney University Web
site, 19
stock
    news sites, 106
    researching, 103-105
        catalysts, 104
        comparisons, 104
        fundamentals, 104

price history, 104
price target, 104
stock markets, *Money* magazine, 9-10
trading, 107-110
Syracuse University Web site, 86

T

Tax Analysts Online Web site, 87
Tax Sites Web site, 88
taxes, 77
    accountants, finding, 88
        Accountant-Search
        Web site, 89
        California Society of
        CPAs, 88
        Tax Sites Web site, 88
    audits, Syracuse University
        Web site, 86
    electronic filing, 86
    example impacts of stock
        sales, 84-85
    Fairmark Press Web site, 79
    forms, downloading, 81-82
    Internal Revenue Service
        (IRS) Web site, 80
    long-term gains, 83
    Money magazine, 11
    online calculators, 85
    online warnings, 78
    questions and answers
        Tax Analysts Online
        Web site, 87
        TaxWeb Web site, 87
    short-term gains, 83
    SmartMoney Web site
        capital gains taxes, 79
        retirement taxes, 79

Third Age Web site, 171
trading stock, 107-110
transaction sites, 21-22

U

U.S. News & World Report magazine Web site, 150
university sites, 18-20

V

vendor sites, 23
viewing real estate, 142-145
Virtual Relocation Web site, 130

W–Z

Web sites
  Accountant-Search, 89
  American Academy of Estate
    Planning Attorneys, 192
  American Bankers
    Association, 29
  American Council of Life
    Insurance, 65
  American Savings Education
    Council, 170
  Bank of America, 37
  Bankrate, 51, 137
  calculators, 23
  California Society of
    CPAs, 88
  CBS MarketWatch, 106
  College Board, 158
  College Parents of
    America, 163
  College Savings Plan
    Network, 154
  community sites, 18
  Countrywide Home
    Loans, 134
  Credit Information Center, 52
  Deloitte & Touche, 193

DivorceSource, 125
E*Trade, 21
eStudentLoan, 161
Fairmark Press, 79
Family Money magazine, 33,
  123
FundAlarm, 101
Gomez Advisors, 39
Green, 20
Homefair, 133
Hoover's Online, 107
Independent Insurance
  Agents of America, 66
Insurance Information
  Institute, 64
Insurance News Network, 72
Internal Revenue Service
  (IRS), 80
iVillage, 54
Life Advice Library, 118
LifeNet, 191
LoanWeb, 138
Love At Home, 118
MetLife, 23
Money magazine, 8
Morningstar, 99
Mortgagebot, 140
MSN MoneyCentral, 15
Mutual Fund Connection,
  102
National Association
  Investors Corporation, 95
National Association of
  Student Financial Aid
  Administrators, 155
Pimco Innovation Fund, 101
Quicken, 34, 169
Raging Bull, 111
Relocation Central, 129
RetireNet, 176
SaveWealth, 182
Senior Resource, 73
SmartMoney University, 19
Syracuse University, 86

Tax Analysts Online, 87
Tax Sites, 88
TaxWeb, 87
Third Age, 171
transaction sites, 21-22
U.S. News & World Report
  magazine, 150
university sites, 18-20
vendor sites, 23
Virtual Relocation, 130
Wells Fargo Bank, 56
WillWorks, 188
Wingspan Bank, 42
wills, 181-189
    American Academy of Estate
    Planning Attorneys, 192

chat rooms, 187
Deloitte & Touche Web
  site, 193
estate planning quiz, 185
estate taxes, 189-190
LifeNet Web site, 191
living trusts, 193
Nolo Press Web site, 183
powers of attorney, 184
probate, 184
Quicken Web site, 187
SaveWealth Web site, 182
taxes, 192
WillWorks Web site, 188
Wingspan Bank Web site, 42

Tell Us What You Think!

As the reader of this book, *you* are our most important critic and commentator. We value your opinion and want to know what we're doing right, what we could do better, what areas you'd like to see us publish in, and any other words of wisdom you're willing to pass our way.

You can email or write me directly to let me know what you did or didn't like about this book—as well as what we can do to make our books stronger.

Please note that I cannot help you with technical problems related to the topic of this book, and that due to the high volume of mail I receive, I might not be able to reply to every message.

When you write, please be sure to include this book's title and author as well as your name and phone or fax number. I will carefully review your comments and share them with the author and editors who worked on the book.

Email: *internet_sams@mcp.com*

Mail: Mark Taber
          Associate Publisher
          Sams Publishing
          201 West 103rd Street
          Indianapolis, IN 46290 USA

SAMS Teach Yourself Today

e-Banking

Managing your money and transactions online

Brian Nixon and Mary Dixon
ISBN: 0-672-31882-2
$17.99 US/ $26.95 CAN

Other Sams Teach Yourself Today Titles

e-Parenting
Evelyn and Karin Petersen
ISBN: 0-672-31818-0
$17.99 US/ $26.95 CAN

e-Music
Brandon Barber
ISBN: 0-672-31855-5
$17.99 US/ $26.95 CAN

e-Real Estate
Jack Segner
ISBN: 0-672-31815-6
$17.99 US/ $26.95 CAN

e-Job Hunting
Eric Schlesinger and Susan Musich
ISBN: 0-672-31817-2
$17.99 US/ $26.95 CAN

e-Auctions
Preston Gralla
ISBN: 0-672-31819-9
$17.99 US/ $26.95 CAN

e-Trading
Tiernan Ray
ISBN: 0-672-31821-0
$17.99 US/ $26.95 CAN

SAMS — All prices are subject to change.

www.samspublishing.com